Bill Hylton's
Power-Tool
JOINERY

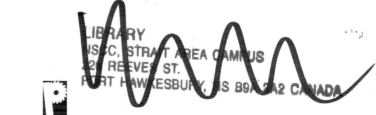

POPULAR WOODWORKING BOOKS
CINCINNATI, OHIO
www.popularwoodworking.com

READ THIS IMPORTANT SAFETY NOTICE

To prevent accidents, keep safety in mind while you work. Use the safety guards installed on power equipment; they are for your protection. When working on power equipment, keep fingers away from saw blades, wear safety goggles to prevent injuries from flying wood chips and sawdust, wear headphones to protect your hearing and consider installing a dust vacuum to reduce the amount of airborne sawdust in your woodshop. Don't wear loose clothing, such as neckties or shirts with loose sleeves, or jewelry, such as rings, necklaces or bracelets, when working on power equipment. Tie back long hair to prevent it from getting caught in your equipment. People who are sensitive to certain chemicals should check the chemical content of any product before using it. The authors and editors who compiled this book have tried to make the contents as accurate and correct as possible. Plans, illustrations, photographs and text have been carefully checked. All instructions, plans and projects should be carefully read, studied and understood before beginning construction. Due to the variability of local conditions, construction materials, skill levels, etc., neither the author nor Popular Woodworking Books assumes any responsibility for any accidents, injuries, damages or other losses incurred resulting from the material presented in this book. Prices listed for supplies and equipment were current at the time of publication and are subject to change. Glass shelving should have all edges polished and must be tempered. Untempered glass shelves may shatter and can cause serious bodily injury. Tempered shelves are very strong and if they break, will only crumble, minimizing personal injury.

METRIC CONVERSION CHART

to convert	to	multiply by
Inches	Centimeters	2.54
Centimeters	Inches	0.4
Feet	Centimeters	30.5
Centimeters	Feet	0.03
Yards	Meters	0.9
Meters	Yards	1.1
Sq. Inches	Sq. Centimeters	6.45
Sq. Centimeters	Sq. Inches	0.16
Sq. Feet	Sq. Meters	0.09
Sq. Meters	Sq. Feet	10.8
Sq. Yards	Sq. Meters	0.8
Sq. Meters	Sq. Yards	1.2
Pounds	Kilograms	0.45
Kilograms	Pounds	2.2
Ounces	Grams	28.4
Grams	Ounces	0.035

Bill Hylton's Power-Tool Joinery. Copyright © 2005 by Bill Hylton. Printed and bound in China. All rights reserved. No part of this book may be reproduced in any form or by any electronic or mechanical means including information storage and retrieval systems without permission in writing from the publisher, except by a reviewer, who may quote brief passages in a review. Published by Popular Woodworking Books, an imprint of F&W Publications, Inc., 4700 East Galbraith Road, Cincinnati, Ohio, 45236. First edition.

Visit our Web site at www.popularwoodworking.com for information on more resources for woodworkers.

Other fine Popular Woodworking Books are available from your local bookstore or direct from the publisher.

09   08   07   06   05   5   4   3   2   1

Library of Congress Cataloging-in-Publication Data

Hylton, William H.
   Bill Hylton's power-tool joinery / Bill Hylton.
     p.   cm.
   Includes index.
   ISBN 1-55870-738-7 (pbk.: alk. paper)
   ISBN 1-55870-766-2 (Hardcover: alk. paper)
   1. Woodwork.   2. Joinery.   3. Power tools.   I. Title: Power-tool joinery   II. Title.
TT185.H9   2005
684'.083--dc22   2004027514

ACQUISITIONS EDITOR: Jim Stack
EDITOR: Amy Hattersley
DESIGNER: Brian Roeth
TECHNICAL ILLUSTRATIONS: Jim Stack
PRODUCTION COORDINATOR: Jennifer Wagner

fw
F•W PUBLICATIONS, INC.

Photo credit: Ned Hylton

ABOUT THE AUTHOR

Bill Hylton is a longtime woodworker and woodworking writer. He writes a column on Power Tool Joinery for *Popular Woodworking* magazine and is a frequent contributor to *Woodworker's Journal*. He has written many woodworking books, including *Illustrated Cabinetmaking, Router Magic, Country Pine, Woodworking with the Router* (with Fred Matlack), *Handcrafted Shelves and Cabinets* (with Amy Rowland) and *Chests of Drawers*.

ACKNOWLEDGEMENTS

I acknowledge up front that I didn't write this entire book all by myself with no help from anybody. I know you are shocked. Shocked! But that's the way it is.

I'm indebted to a long list of people who inched me toward this project.

Several years ago, Steve Shanesy and Chris Schwarz of *Popular Woodworking* magazine, spurred by ad director Don Schroder, a friend and former colleague, gave me an opportunity to write a regular column on power-tool joinery. The column, of course, provided a huge mound of grist for this book.

A friend, neighbor, and former officemate, Ken Burton, author of *Cutting-Edge Tables Saw Tips & Tricks*, put me in touch with Jim Stack of Popular Woodworking Books. Jim accepted my proposal for this book, and he and his colleagues helped worm the book out of me.

I'm indebted to my friend Donna Chiarelli, a professional photographer, for her photographic guidance, advice and tips — all sound and all free. I'm also indebted to Mr. Tripod and Mr. Self-Timer for their invaluable assistance in doing the photography. (Too bad they aren't more helpful around the woodshop.)

Editor Amy Hattersley pried copy and visuals from me and wouldn't let me get too far off schedule. After all my words and photos and drawings on the topic were turned in, Jim Stack dove into the morass and extricated the book you hold in your hands. Good work, Jim!

I won't go into the whole grim business of how I toiled with this book. Suffice it to say, the love and support and, yes, the occasional tart remark and ongoing forbearance of my wife, Judi, was essential. Thanks honey.

CONTENTS

CHAPTER ONE
edge joints . . . *8*

CHAPTER TWO
dado joints . . . *18*

CHAPTER SIX
sliding dovetail joints . . . *60*

CHAPTER SEVEN
dovetails . . . *72*

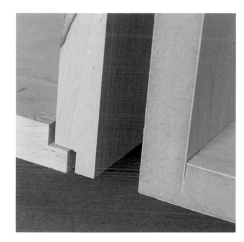

CHAPTER THREE
rabbet joints . . . *30*

CHAPTER FOUR
miter joints . . . *39*

CHAPTER FIVE
splined joints . . . *50*

CHAPTER EIGHT
half-lap joints . . . *81*

CHAPTER NINE
**mortise-and-tenon
joints** . . . *93*

CHAPTER TEN
biscuitry . . . *114*

INTRODUCTION

This book is a basic joint-cutting manual. It tells — and shows — how to cut the fundamental tried-and-true woodworking joints.

When I first started doing woodworking, about a quarter century ago, I had the notion that hand tools were the way to do it. A more pure form. It didn't take very long to grasp that power tools are a whole lot more efficient for most jobs. Not only are they easier and faster to use, but more accurate as well.

With hand tools, each cut is dependent on the accuracy of your layout, on your steadiness of hand, on your fine-motor skills and your strength and stamina. With power tools, on the other hand, the machine setup or a jig or fixture often eliminates the need for marking layout on individual parts, allowing you to knock out cut after uniform cut in part after part.

So face it. I did. Power tools are practical.

Moreover, the power tools I use are the fundamental ones: a table saw and routers, primarily. There are exceptions, of course. A biscuit joiner, for example, is the only practical tool for making biscuit joints. The tool was invented to make the joint, and without it, the joint wouldn't exist.

The emphasis here is on practical joinery. You'll learn how to select a joint that's appropriate for your application, several ways to cut it and how to assemble it.

You'll find chapters on dadoes, rabbets, miters, mortises and tenons, half-blind dovetails and several other fundamental joints. These are the joints whose history is testament to their usefulness. Visit a good museum and study the old furniture; you'll see that these joints are what hold that 250-year-old chest or chair together.

A couple of chapters look closely at industrial-age joints. The lock miter, the drawer lock, the biscuit joint. While they lack the centuries-old tradition, these joints have a long-enough history to warrant respect. And they're strictly machine cut.

Everything in this book is shop tested. Not all the techniques and approaches discussed are personal favorites, but I've tried them and know they work. In explaining "how" to make a cut, I also try to explain "why." How to do a job may be easier to assimilate if you grasp why it's being done a certain way. And knowing why may lead you to another way that's better for you — maybe better period. Which leads me to the next point.

There's always more than one way to handle a task. I have tried pretty conscientiously to present more than one way to cut every joint. For example, cutting rabbets on the

What is original, I think, is the logical, thorough, in-depth presentation. As a basic operating manual, the book has to cover those solid, traditional techniques, as well as newer approaches. Likewise, the information must be easy to find, complete and clearly presented. It has to be down to earth and practical.

table saw is pretty straightforward. You can do it with an everyday blade. But for a lot of rabbets, you might benefit from using a dado cutter in the saw. I explain the ins and outs of that procedure. You can also do the job with a router, running the portable tool across the stock or running the stock across a router table. All of these techniques are in here.

I've included plans for jigs and fixtures that will help you cut individual joints accurately, safely and with less hassle. Sure, you can open your wallet and buy some version of a lot of these jigs. But why buy a jig if you can make it? You are a woodworker, aren't you?

It won't shock you to learn that none of this info is really original. Cutting a dado is cutting a dado. Usually, the best techniques are the tried-and-true ones.

When you have a question, when you can't remember an operation's exact sequence of steps, you'll be able to quickly flip to the proper page.

A basic operating manual is exactly what I've produced here; a systematic, thorough guidebook to cutting joints. Here, you'll find an index and cross references. Cutting laps is a lot like cutting tenons, for example, so you'll find cross references from one chapter to another where such references are pertinent.

Finally, let me emphasize that using power tools isn't risk free. While all the techniques I've described here are things I've done repeatedly and consider to be safe, none are foolproof. Ultimately, you are the one at risk, and you have to decide before you try something whether or not you are comfortable doing it.

EDGE JOINTS

The edge joint may be the fundamental joint
in woodworking.

Anytime you need a solid-wood panel
that's more than 6" or 8" wide, you create it
by gluing two or more narrow boards edge to
edge. Casework, tabletops, door panels, drawer fronts, shelves, headboards and footboards
all require boards or panels of a width that
outstrips available stock and the capacity of
shop machinery.

Butted Edge Joint

The most widely used edge joint couldn't be simpler: two boards with straight, square edges and some glue. Experts agree that a properly fitted glue joint is stronger than the wood itself. If you cut and assemble this joint right, the individual boards will split before the joint does.

So why are there so many more complicated variations — splines, biscuits, interlocking profiles — on the simple edge joint?

Some woodworkers just can't accept that a simple joint is better than one that incorporates a bit of the mechanical.

Sometimes, though, a more complex joint is warranted. For instance, splines or biscuits used to align the mating boards during assembly. This use is legitimate, especially if your means to flatten a broad panel are limited. Having one board just a skosh high or low in a glued up panel can mean a long session with either a hand plane or a noisy, dusty belt sander.

What I'll focus on here is how to produce a good, simple, butted edge joint. In addition, I'll talk about the tongue-and-groove joint, since it is used almost exclusively as an edge-to-edge joint.

Splines and biscuits are used often in edge-to-edge joinery, of course, but they're also used in other configurations — edge-to-face, end-to-face, and so forth. Each of these uses merits its own chapter.

Basic edge joints

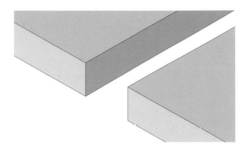

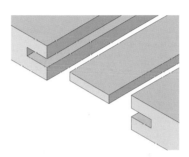

Butt joint

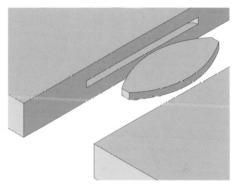

Splined joint

Biscuit joint

Tongue-and-groove joint

Routed glue joint

Used for everything from tabletops to chest lids or to cabinet sides, wide panels are common in woodworking. To get them, we simply have to glue the too-narrow boards we have edge to edge.

ASSEMBLY

Assemble your panel on a flat surface. If your assembly table is bowed or twisted, you'll have difficulty creating a flat glue-up. If all else fails, spread some Kraft paper or newspaper over your table saw (to protect it from glue drips) and do the assembly on it.

Do a dry run before opening the glue. Set out the clamps, position the boards and your cauls and run through the clamp-up. The joints must close with only moderate clamp pressure. If you have to crank the clamps to close the joints, you really need to rejoint the edges before going any further.

I like to use an odd number of clamps. I always begin tightening with the center one and work my way out, alternating from one side of center to the other. To keep the panel flat, I set alternating clamps across the top surface of the panel.

Spread the glue, set the boards on the bottom-side clamps and place the top-side clamps. As you tighten each clamp, make sure the faces are flush by rubbing your finger across the seam between boards at that clamp. Tug up or push down on the ends of individual boards as needed to make them flush.

If you feel uncomfortable monitoring two or three seams at one time (something you have to do if you're gluing up three or four boards), you can handle the glue-up in stages. Do two glue-ups of two boards each. Wait a half hour or so for the glue to set up, then do a third glue-up that joins them into one wide panel.

Whether you are gluing up butted, biscuited, splined or routed edge joints, the assembly process follows the same basic routine.

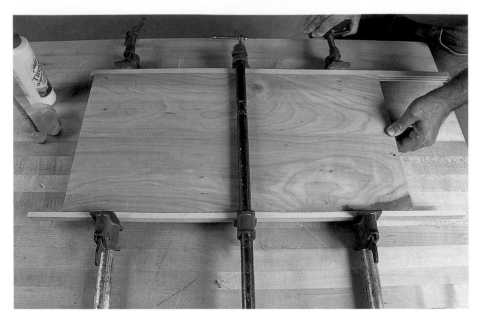

Glue a panel with clamps across both the top and bottom to keep the assembly flat. Use enough clamps to spread pressure across the entire joint. I tighten the middle clamp first, then work out from there, alternating from right to left, until all the clamps are tight.

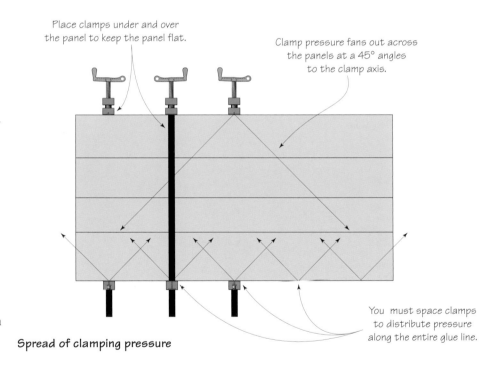

Place clamps under and over the panel to keep the panel flat.

Clamp pressure fans out across the panels at a 45° angles to the clamp axis.

You must space clamps to distribute pressure along the entire glue line.

Spread of clamping pressure

Skimping on clamps can weaken a joint. Here's why: If only three clamps are used on this panel — one in the middle, one at each end — only the center joint gets uniform pressure along its entire length. Each flanking joint has two spots that don't get pressure, which diminishes the bond. In this instance, five clamps are needed. As you plan a glue-up, visualize the spread of pressure and clamp accordingly.

TONGUE-AND-GROOVE JOINT

A traditional edge-to-edge joint, the tongue and groove is just what its name implies. The edge of one board has a groove. The edge of the mating board has a tongue. The tongue goes into the groove, and the boards are joined. The resulting edge joint has a mechanical interlock.

The tongue-and-groove joint's many applications show up often in building construction: strip flooring and paneling most notably. The tongue-and-groove is even used on sheet goods intended for subflooring and for exterior siding. The boards or panels butt edge-to-edge quickly, creating a flush surface.

Seldom is this type of joint glued. While it can be glued, that isn't the common way to assemble it. It's usually used where the mating boards are attached to another surface or a frame. That way, the boards can expand and contract without adverse effect. You can run fasteners through the root of the tongue and the mating board will conceal them. Another aspect to this aesthetic is that the boards can shrink without opening the joint enough to expose whatever is behind it.

In furniture-making, the tongue-and-groove joint is excellent for edge-to-edge glue-ups. If cut precisely, the joint ensures that the faces of adjoining boards come flush easily and that they can't creep out of alignment as you position and tighten clamps — no tugging on boards, no extra clamps on the ends of seams forcing the boards into a flush alignment.

Better yet, when the clamps come off, a little scraping and light sanding is all that's need to ready the panel for the next step.

CUTTING THE JOINT

Consider the design of the joint before you set up to cut it. Good proportions are essential to produce a strong joint, but the intent of the joint enters into

Tongue-and-groove stock (center) is readily available at most building centers. Though functional, its edge-to-edge joint doesn't fit nearly as well as the sort you cut yourself. The top example is scaled for a glue-free application, where the individual boards are free to expand and contract. The boards can shrink without having the tongue completely withdraw from the groove. The bottom joint is scaled for a glue-up, where the tongue-and-groove serves primarily to align the faces.

the equation as well.

Start with convention. A piece of 1×8 tongue-and-groove pine from the lumberyard has about a ⅜" deep groove. This is a good proportion for the material and its anticipated applications. It'll be assembled with fasteners (nails through the shoulder of the tongue) rather than glue. The material will be able to expand and contract without opening the joint.

The general rule says you should have a square tongue that's roughly one third of the stock thickness and centered on the edge. Working with ¾" stock, that plays out to a ¼"-thick by ¼"-long tongue. And a matching groove, of course.

A longer tongue — one that's ½" long, for example — is prone to break at the shoulder. Likewise, the walls of a deep groove may crack.

But a tongue-and-groove for a panel glue-up — just to register and align the faces — requires only a vestigial

tongue. One-eighth inch is all it takes.

The joint should be a firm press fit: If you have to knock the pieces together, then struggle to pull them apart, the joint's too tight. Moreover, a tongue that's a hair too fat for the groove may actually seat, but it will stress the groove sidewalls and may, over time, prompt them to split away.

On the other hand, you don't want the tongue to rattle in the groove. This is especially true where the joint is intended to register and align the faces during assembly.

You can cut tongue-and-groove joints with any of several power tools: table saw, shaper or router, either handheld or table-mounted. The focus here is on the table saw and the router.

There's no hard rule on which element of the joint you cut first. I prefer to make the groove first, because I think it's easier to fit the tongue to it than the other way around. If you opt for the opposite, that's fine.

ON THE TABLE SAW

To produce a tongue and groove on the table saw, use a dado cutter rather than your everyday blade (unless your stock is $\frac{3}{8}$" or less in thickness). I use the two outside cutters to produce a $\frac{1}{4}$" cut width when working $\frac{3}{4}$" stock. Thicker stock calls for a wider groove, so set up your dado cutter accordingly.

Set the cutter height next. I'd say that $\frac{1}{2}$" is pressing your luck, and $\frac{1}{4}$" to $\frac{3}{8}$" is optimal for a joint that will be assembled without glue. If you are making a glue joint, remember that a very shallow groove is all you need — $\frac{1}{8}$" or so.

Bring the rip fence into position, positioning it to center the groove on the working stock. Make a test cut and measure the groove shoulders with dial calipers. If your rip fence allows, adjust the position as needed to exactly center the cut. To be practical, get the fence setting as close as possible, then center the cut by making two passes on each board.

When you are content with the cut samples — content in terms of depth and placement — cut a groove on each workpiece.

Switching to the tongue-forming setup is simply a matter of moving the fence. No changes in the cutter or cutter height are necessary. Use a sample groove to position the fence, aligning the outside edge of the cutter with the edge of the sample's groove. It's not unlikely that the dado cutter will conflict with the fence. A sacrificial facing is probably in order. I have such a facing for this, for rabbeting and for a few other jobs. I secure it to the fence with what I call a fence hook. (See the drawing on the next page.)

Cut a tongue on a sample of the working stock, and fit it to the groove. Slide the work along the fence, cutting one shoulder, then spin the work around and repeat the cut to form the second shoulder. Adjust the fence position as necessary to get a good fit.

Now that the setup is dialed in, you can cut the tongues.

Scale the tongue to the application. To align individual boards in a wide glue-up, only a short tongue (left) is needed. If the joint will not be glued and the individual boards will be free to move, a longer tongue is in order. The tongue on the right is about as big as you'll want to go. The center tongue is a good all-purpose proportion.

When setting up the table saw to cut the groove half of the joint, simply eyeball the rip fence position. I sight down across the end of the stock and align a center line drawn on it with the center of the cutter. It probably won't be perfect, but a two-pass work routine centers the groove and eliminates the need for test cuts, measurements and microadjustments at this stage.

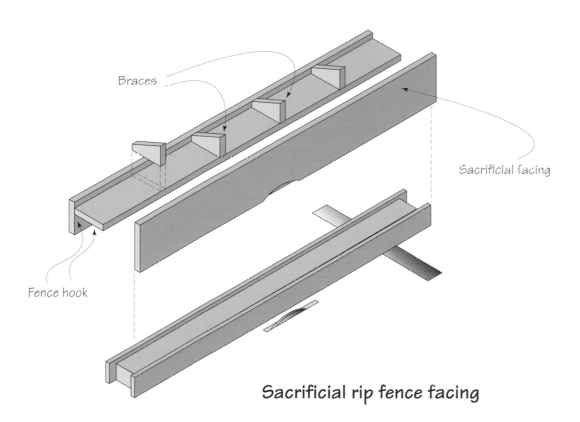

Braces

Sacrificial facing

Fence hook

Sacrificial rip fence facing

Are you doing a lot of table-saw rabbeting with a dado head? Working with a moulding head? A sacrificial facing for the fence protects both the fence and the cutter. This drop-in-place design requires a few strips of scrap plywood and 15 minutes of cutting and assembling. Setup is fast, and no clamps obstruct the cutting path.

A sacrificial facing on the rip fence preserves the dado cutter and the fence, yet allows for some cut width adjustment using the fence position. You can clamp a scrap to the fence, but often the clamps get in the way of the cut. I made a keeper that straddles the fence; one out-of-the-way clamp immobilizes it.

Use a grooved piece to set the fence for the tongue cuts. Align the outermost cutter tooth with the inner wall of the groove. A test cut and some fine-tuning may be required at this stage to fit the joint properly.

WITH A ROUTER

Using a router gives you other options, both in terms of the approach and the cutters.

Specifically, you can do the work on the router table, and move the boards across the tool. Or you can plant the boards and move a portable router across them.

If you are going to use the former approach, you can cut tongue-and-groove joints with a straight bit, a slot cutter or a dedicated tongue and groove cutter assembly or set. If you want to use a portable router, I recommend using the slot cutter.

Using a Straight Bit: There are pros and cons to using a straight bit. On the plus side, a straight bit is a commonplace bit that has a multiplicity of applications. You probably already have one.

On the negative side, you may, depending on the hardness of your stock, need to make more than one pass per cut to reach the full depth. That can trigger work sequence woes, especially on a job that entails a lot of workpieces. Specifically, you have to make a pass on each workpiece, adjust the cut depth, then make a second pass on each piece. That's a lot of handling.

Somewhere between pro and con is the fact that, practically speaking, the straight bit is a tongue-and-groove cutter only in a table-mounted router. Using it in a portable router requires balancing the tool on narrow edges, a tough assignment.

Cutting tongues and grooves on the router table with a straight bit mimics using a dado cutter on the table saw.

The cut controls are these: The bit's extension above the tabletop governs the tongue length/groove depth. Fence position controls lateral placement of the cut. With the work on edge, face tight against the fence, cut both elements.

The setup sequence and cutting routine follow those of the table saw

A rabbet cut into each edge of the board forms the tongue. It's a good idea to cut a sample and check its fit before cutting all of the boards.

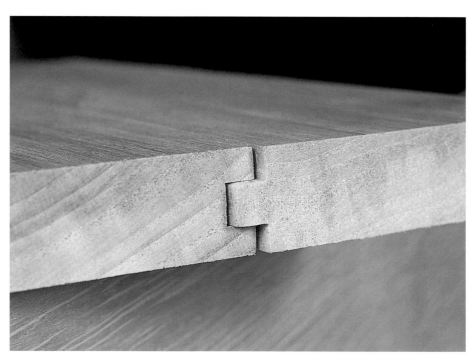

approach:

- Install the bit and set its extension.
- Position the fence for the grooving cut.
- Rout the grooves, centering them most easily by making two passes.
- Reposition the fence for the tongue cuts.
- Rout the tongue by making two passes on each workpiece.

A snug press-fit is your goal. You lose the registration benefit if the fit is loose and stress the groove walls if the fit is too tight. This is a first try — honest!

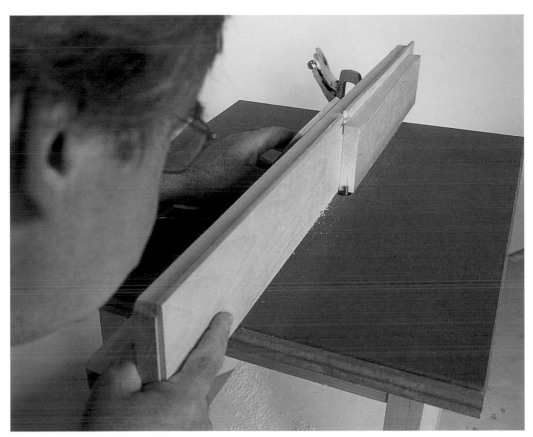

Setting the router table fence for grooving with a straight bit generally is the same for setting up the table saw. With one end of the fence secured, swing the free end to align the centerline on a sample workpiece with the bit's center. Note that both the fence and the tabletop have auxiliary coverings to downsize or eliminate the bit openings, thus forestalling workpiece hangups.

Using a Slot Cutter: The slot cutter is another generic bit that produces tongue-and-groove joints without a lot of fuss. It works equally well in table-mounted and portable routers.

It, too, comes with both pros and cons. On the positive side, it will cut a full-depth groove easily. It is a good choice for thin stock, since a variety of slot widths under ¼" are available. Flip that coin, however, and you find there aren't single cutters available in widths greater than ¼". To produce a groove that's wider than ¼" requires an assembly with two or more cutters on its arbor.

The primary difference between the slot cutter and the straight bit is in the way the cut placement is controlled and the workpiece orientation. The tongue length/groove depth is controlled by the pilot bearing or the fence, while the position of the cuts on the edge of the work is controlled by the bit extension adjustment. All the cuts are made with the work flat on the tabletop or with the router on the face

of the board.

Start by cutting the groove. Rest the stock flat on the tabletop by the cutter, and raise or lower the cutter until its tip is centered on the stock's edge. Adjust the fence for the desired depth of cut. Feed the stock across the tabletop, its edge tight against the fence, to make the cut.

As with the straight bit, you can use a two-pass approach to center the groove. Make one pass with the face against the tabletop, the second with the back against the tabletop. The groove will be slightly wider than ¼", most likely, but it'll be centered.

When you switch the setup for cutting the tongues, leave the fence setting alone. Lay your grooved sample beside the bit and lower it until the cutting tip aligns with the groove wall that's closest to the tabletop. (You don't want to trap the work between the cutter and the tabletop.)

Cut a test tongue and adjust the setup as necessary to fit the tongue to the grooves. Then cut away!

When you're using a straight bit, repositioning the fence for cutting tongues can be an optical challenge. Sight across the bit to the grooved sample to make an initial setting. Cut a sample tongue, check how it fits the groove and adjust the fence position if necessary. Note that the cut is on the fence side of the work.

The tongue-and-groove joint requires preciseness of fit rather than preciseness of dimension. As with other setups, I eyeball the slot cutter elevation in relation to a center line marked on a work sample. The groove is centered using the two-pass work sequence, and the exact groove width is only marginally relevant.

Use the fence rather than the slotter's pilot bearing to govern the depth of the groove. Typically, you can establish this using the eyeball method — rather than precise measurement — since the same fence position is used for both grooving and tongue-forming cuts.

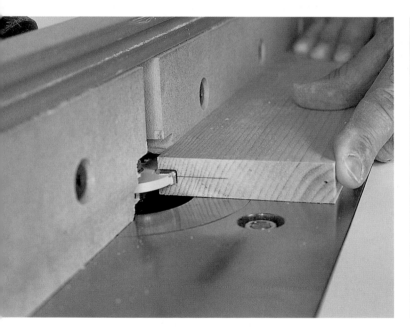

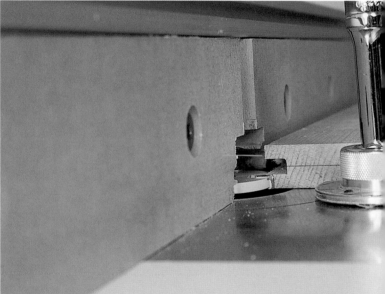

With a slot cutter, the work rests flat on the tabletop throughout the cut. Center the cut accurately in the usual way: make passes referencing both faces. The second pass will probably widen the groove slightly, but it also will center the groove.

Always make the tongue-forming cuts with the cutter lowered to the table, rather than trapping the work between it and the table. As with the other tool setups, use a grooved sample for the initial setting. (This table has a router lift that features a topside adjuster.)

Dedicated Tongue and Groove Cutters: Most bit manufacturers sell individual bits or sets of bits designed specifically for cutting tongue and groove joints. Most of them give you two separate bits: one for cutting the grooves, the other for the tongue. The benefits of the sets are these:

• You shouldn't have to "fit" the tongue to the groove. Out of the box, the cutters should produce the optimally fitted joint. Provided the bits have sufficient capacity to work stock more than ¾" thick, and provided you mark a reference — and mind the marks as you work — having the groove and tongue off-center shouldn't be a problem.

• You can mill stock in a real production mode by setting up two router tables, one for each bit. The tables don't have to be elaborate.

In addition, you can find at least one adjustable set, which allows you to vary the groove width (and tongue thickness, of course) according to the dictates of different joints. One-piece bits and assemblies cost a little less. You can even find one that will chamfer the shoulders as it cuts the joint.

Unless you do a lot of tongue-and-groove joinery, I don't consider these dedicated cutters as worthwhile investments.

Profiling the Joint: The V-groove, or tiny bead often seen on a tongue-and-groove joint, is camouflage meant to disguise a gap that opens seasonally as the wood expands and contracts.

The V-groove, if you opt for it, is created by cutting a chamfer along the grooved edge of the board, as well as along the shoulder of the tongue. When the joint is assembled, the chamfers come together in the V-groove. If you opt for this embellishment, you can buy a bit that will mill the chamfers at the same time it cuts the tongue or the groove.

You can also cut the chamfers on

Traditional tongue-and-groove cutters offer two-pass joint-making. A single pass with the groover (right) produces the groove. A pass with the tongue-cutter (left) yields the complete tongue — offset if necessary to match an off-center groove.

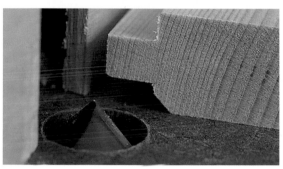

To embellish a joint with a V-groove, chamfer both the grooved edge and the shoulder of the tongue. Make both cuts with a V-groove bit. The trick is to get the same chamfer width on both edge and shoulder so the "assembled" V-groove is symmetrical.

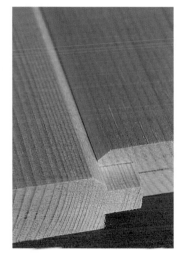

A beaded joint is cut with an edge-beading bit in a table-mounted router. Cut the shoulder of the tongue, not the groove edge. Adjust the cut so you get the same width of quirk on either side of the bead.

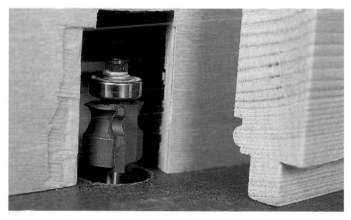

the router table using a common V-groover. It simply requires additional operations. Cut the grooved-edge chamfer, then shift the fence slightly to position the work for the cut at the tongue.

If you want the bead to dress up your joint, use a small edge-beading bit. The cut must be placed at the shoulder of the tongue. If you cut it along the grooved edge, it will weaken the groove sidewall, and the groove could easily split off. Because of the tongue, the bit has to be elevated pretty far, but it shouldn't present a problem.

A third profile option is to use a small core box or roundnose bit to cut a cove along the shoulder of the tongue. Like the chamfer, the cove can be cut on both edges of the joint to produce a groove profile.

DADO JOINTS

In casework of any size and material, the dado is the joinery of choice. It follows that ancient woodworking adage, "Use the simplest joint that will work."

The dado certainly works, and it has stood the test of time, too, with its centuries-long history of use in cabinetmaking.

It definitely is simple. All the dado joint variations derive from the cut itself. A dado is a flat-bottomed channel cut that crosses the grain of the wood. (When it runs with the grain, the channel is called a groove.) One board gets a dado, or groove, and the mating board fits into it. One well-placed, properly sized cut makes the joint, and with today's power tools, it's a cut that's almost trivial to make.

The dado does not have to be deep to create a strong joint. One-eighth inch is deep enough in solid wood, $\frac{1}{4}$" in plywood, MDF or particleboard. This shallow channel helps align the parts during assembly, and the ledge it creates is enough to support the weight of a shelf and everything loaded on it. The dado also prevents the shelf from cupping.

The one stress it doesn't resist effectively is tension. It won't prevent the shelf from pulling out of the side, for example. Only glue or fasteners can do that. Because all of the gluing surfaces involve end grain, the glue strength is limited.

The principal dado joints reflect the character of the dado cut: through, stopped and blind.

When the dado extends from edge to edge, it's a through dado, an easy dado to cut. The most common objection to it in a joint is that it shows. A face frame or trim covering the case edges conceals the joint, however.

A dado or groove doesn't have to be through, of course. It can begin at one edge and end before it reaches the other (stopped), or it can begin and end shy of either edge (blind). These are a little trickier to cut.

To make a joint of a stopped or blind dado, the corner(s) of the mating board must be notched, creating a projection that fits in the dado. Sizing the notches so you have a little play from end to end makes it easier to align the edges of the parts. But it does sacrifice a bit of the strength that the narrow shoulder imparts.

Cutting Dadoes

There are many ways to successfully cut a dado. It's good to have several techniques in your repertoire, because there isn't one that's best for every situation.

Keep a couple of criteria in mind. To end up with a strong joint, you need to make a cut of the correct width. The bottom needs to be smooth and flat; the sides, perpendicular. If the cut is too wide, glue isn't going to compensate; the joint will be weak. Get the fit right.

The two most obvious power tools for cutting dadoes are the table saw and the router. But there are some other options.

You can make dadoes with a radial-arm saw. If you have this saw and are comfortable with it, you probably can recite its advantages. Fitted with a dado head, the radial-arm saw hogs through dadoes quickly. The workpiece is face up, so you can see what you're doing. Layout marks are visible, and you can line up each cut quickly and accurately. When a stopped dado is needed, you

One is a dado, and one is a groove. Both were cut with the same bit. The cross-grain cut is the dado, the long-grain cut is the groove.

Basic dado joints

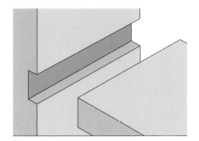

Through dado

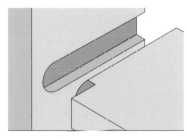

Stopped dado

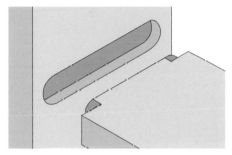

Blind dado

For the optimum joint strength, a dado's width must be just a few thousandths greater than the thickness of the mating piece. The dado on the left is dead on, the center dado just a skosh wide — the mating piece is slightly out of square — the one on the right is obviously too wide.

ADVANCED DADO JOINERY

Once you've mastered dadoing and have used the basic dado joints in your projects, it's a good time to look at some slightly more complicated derivatives.

The first variant you will be tempted to try is the dado and rabbet. The dado you cut is narrower than the thickness of the mating board. You reduce that board's thickness by cutting a rabbet across its end. In terms of theoretical gluing strength, this joint is all end grain to long grain (which isn't good), but in practice, it glues well if the tongue is properly fitted to the dado.

The orientation of the joint is important. The shelf can carry more weight if the rabbet is in the top surface. Otherwise, you risk having the board split below the tongue.

A more labor-intensive variant of the dado and rabbet is the dado and tongue. The dado and tongue offers the advantage if the extra shoulder, which makes the joint more stable and rack resistant. Your instinct may be to center the tongue on the horizontal piece, but you get a stronger joint if you offset the tongue. Orient the wider shoulder to the top, the narrower shoulder to the bottom. You can make either a through or stopped joint. The latter hides shrinkage and gaps.

For MDF and particleboard, which have no grain and none of the strength it imparts, the dado and spline joint is perfect. The spline should penetrate about one-third of the side's thickness and about twice that distance into the horizontal piece. Be judicious with your cuts: You'll weaken the side if you cut into it too deeply. And if you don't cut deep enough into the horizontal piece, you won't gain the strength you want. Offset the spline below the center of the horizontal piece.

Cutting the dadoes you need for this joint is a straightforward proposition. You can groove the ends of the horizontal boards most efficiently on the router table with a slot cutter. Make the cuts with the workpieces flat on the tabletop, their ends butted against the fence.

Advanced dado joints

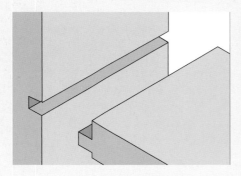

Dado and spline

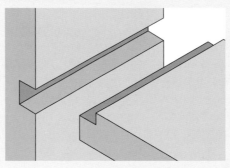

Dado and rabbet

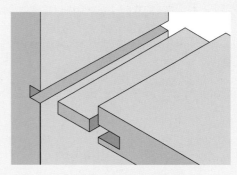

Dado and tongue

can cut to a mark. The work isn't moved during the cut, so the pieces shouldn't twist or shift out of position. This is especially helpful on angled cuts, whether a miter or a bevel (or both).

I have cut dadoes on narrow workpieces using a sliding compound miter saw. Most such saws have a cut-depth adjuster; you set the cut depth, then "waste" each dado with kerf after kerf. It's one of those operations you do once, just to try it. Once was enough for me.

A friend of mine has made dadoes with a 6" dado head in a circular saw. Me? I'm not going there. The table saw and the router give me all the options I need.

Table Saw Dadoes

The table saw is powerful and equipped with accessories — a rip fence and a miter gauge, which are useful in positioning cuts. Like a lot of other woodworkers, I use a shop-made crosscut sled (instead of the miter gauge) for crosscutting, and it also works for dadoes. To use the saw effectively for dadoing, you need a dado cutter (either a stack set or a wobbler).

You can waste a narrow dado pretty quickly with whatever blade is on the saw. If you have a manageable workpiece and just one or two dadoes to cut, make five to seven kerfs to form each one. But to cut a cabinet's worth of dadoes, use a dado cutter.

A typical dado stack set consists of two outside blades, several chippers and washerlike shims. Always use both blades and supplement them with the chippers necessary to produce the desired cut width. The shims allow you to fine-tune the cut width. If you use a particular stack width again and again, make yourself a zero-clearance insert to use with the setup. Doing so both minimizes chipping and is a safer way to work.

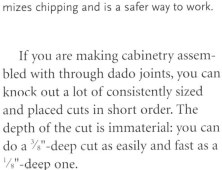

If you are making cabinetry assembled with through dado joints, you can knock out a lot of consistently sized and placed cuts in short order. The depth of the cut is immaterial: you can do a ⅜"-deep cut as easily and fast as a ⅛"-deep one.

What isn't necessarily quick and easy is achieving the precise width of cut you want. Stack sets, which give the cleanest cut, consist of separate blades and chippers. The trick is to select the combination needed to produce the approximate width of cut desired. To tune the set to a precise cut width, insert shims between the elements. This technique involves more trial-and-error than I like.

Some woodworkers (those with too much time on their hands, I think) make a chart or a cut sample with notes on the combinations of blades, chippers and specific shims needed to produce common-width dadoes. If you have the patience for this endeavor, my hat is off to you.

But the woodworkers most likely to use the table saw for dadoing are those who are looking at a lot of cuts and not a lot of time to make them. Often these folks will adopt workarounds to

The rip fence is the first choice for guiding any table saw cut, and dadoes are no exception. The fence allows you to position the cuts consistently from part to part. Setup is fast, simple and accurate, and cuts are made without fuss.

avoid protracted setups. They'll shoot for an undersized dado and plane or sand the part to be housed in it to fit. Or they'll use the dado and rabbet joint (the mating part is rabbeted to form a tongue that fits whatever dado has been cut).

How do you locate and guide the cut? It's tempting to use the rip fence, since it allows you to locate a cut consistently on both sides of a cabinet or bookcase and also eliminates the need for layout. But it isn't a crosscutting guide, and dadoes are crosscuts.

The issue is proportion. If you have a workpiece that's 12" × 24", you can easily guide the 24"-long edge along the rip fence. But it is more tricky to guide the 12"-long edge along the fence. Depending on where you place your hands to feed the work, the panel may tend to "walk" rather than slide. Get it cocked ever so slightly and it may climb up on the cutter and be tossed back at you.

As the proportions of a workpiece swing toward square, the potential for trouble diminishes. Guiding the short dimension of a 24" × 34" base-cabinet side along the rip fence for dadoing cuts is seldom a problem. Nevertheless, I recommend using a crosscut guide for most table-saw dadoing.

Of the two crosscutting guides, I prefer the crosscut sled. It's built specifically for right-angle cuts and rides in both miter-gauge slots (instead of just one). In addition, since the sled is what moves, it effectively immobilizes the workpiece, carrying the stationary workpiece with it. The work doesn't squirm or twist as you push it onto the cutter. Fit the sled with a stop so you can accurately and consistently locate a cut on multiples without individual layouts. (The drawing of the router-table dadoing sled shows a stop accessory that fits on a table saw crosscut sled.)

Dadoes tend to parallel the short dimension of case parts. Workpieces that are too long and narrow to be guided along the fence should be cradled in the miter gauge.

An accurate, shop-made crosscut sled is the best guide accessory to use for dadoing on the table saw. When set on the sled base tight against the fence, the work won't shimmy or shift out of position as you slide the box across the dado cutter.

When a dado or groove doesn't extend completely from one edge of a board to the other, it's referred to as a stopped cut or a blind cut. It can begin at one edge and end before it reaches the other (stopped), or it can begin and end shy of either edge (blind).

Stopped cuts made on the table saw can be problematic and blind cuts made there can be downright hazardous. Because the work conceals the cutter, it's tricky to determine where to stop. One option is to clamp a stick to the outfeed table that stops the workpiece or the cutoff box at just the right spot.

A blind cut would require you to drop the work onto the spinning dado cutter. It's not a routine that I'd recommend.

Any stopped cut done with a dado head will ramp from the bottom of the cut to the surface. You can leave it and simply enlarge the notch in the mating piece, but in so doing, you sacrifice the strength in the joint that comes from a tightly fitted shoulder. Better is to chisel out the ramp.

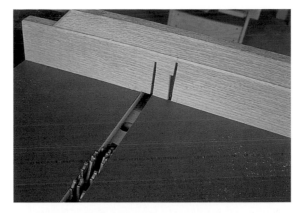

A zero-clearance table-saw insert prevents chipping at the edges of a cut. You can outfit your crosscut sled with a zero-clearance auxiliary bottom using ⅛" hardboard. Set the dado cutter to the desired cut width, then drop the hardboard into the sled and secure it with a few patches of carpet tape. The first cut will divide the hardboard in two and give you a zero-clearance fit at that dado width.

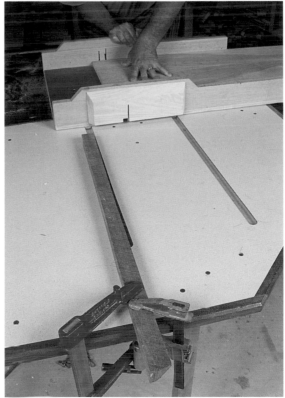

You can safely make a stopped dado on the table saw if you are using a crosscut sled. Clamp a stick to the outfeed table, as shown, so it stops the sled before the cutter breaks through the trailing edge of the work. You'll be able to back the work off the dado head without trouble. The resulting cut will ramp from the dado bottom to the work's face; you'll have to pare out that ramp with a chisel.

Routing Dadoes

The router often is touted as the most versatile tool in the shop, and it certainly is useful for dadoing. The cutters offer convenient sizing: Want a ½"-wide dado? Use a ½" bit. Want a dado for ¾" plywood (which is typically not a full ¾"-thick)? Use a $^{23}/_{32}$" bit. Changing from one bit to another is quick and easy.

The tool also offers options on approach. If you have a router hung in a table, dadoing with it is much like table-saw dadoing. The router, however, gives you the option of moving the tool on a stationary workpiece; in many situations, this is the better approach.

On the Router Table

For a long time, I believed you could rout grooves on a router table more easily than dadoes. Consider the typical router table setup. It's small in comparison to the typical table saw, which has expansive infeed and outfeed tables. So I'd tell woodworkers to limit themselves to small parts, things like drawer sides.

Guided by the fence alone, you can easily rout grooves, since grain typically parallel's a board's long dimension. But try guiding the workpiece's short dimension edge along the fence, or locating a dado 16" from that edge, or 24" or 30". Maneuvering a 6'-long bookcase side or a 24" × 36" base cabinet side on a router table top is a Keystone Kops routine. But a drawer side — if the piece is small and the dado (for the drawer back) is close to the end — can be routed pretty easily. Use a square-ended push block to keep the work square to the fence as you feed it, and to back up the cut.

It might seem that large case parts are best done on the table saw or with a hand-held router. Recently, however, I made a crosscut sled-like accessory for my big router table. The dadoing

The typical router table setup works for dadoing parts like drawer sides. A push block — just a square scrap — stabilizes the work and backs up the cut, preventing tearout as the bit emerges from the cut.

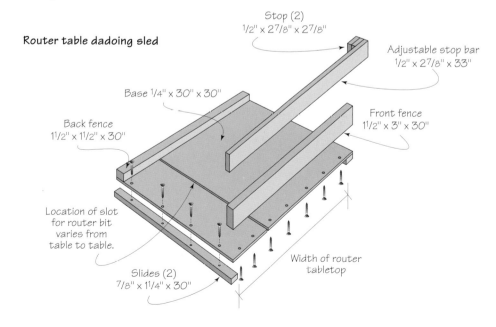

Router table dadoing sled

Stop (2)
1/2" x 27/8" x 27/8"

Adjustable stop bar
1/2" x 27/8" x 33"

Base 1/4" x 30" x 30"

Front fence
11/2" x 3" x 30"

Back fence
11/2" x 11/2" x 30"

Location of slot for router bit varies from table to table.

Slides (2)
7/8" x 11/4" x 30"

Width of router tabletop

sled is guided by the tabletop's edges (see the drawing). I've dadoed some pretty large workpieces with it; the setup was simple, the operation downright easy and the results were clean and precise.

It's changing my attitude, I must say. It offers all the advantages of the table-saw crosscut sled setup but eliminates the irritating (to me, anyway) confrontation with the stack set.

You do need to use a stop to position the work, because the stop also prevents the bit from moving the work. A table-mounted router's bit spins counterclockwise, and it will pull work to the right. You place the stop on the right to counteract that dynamic. (It's the equivalent of positioning the fence on the right.)

The stop has the secondary function of positioning cuts consistently from workpiece to workpiece.

Let me qualify all this by emphasizing that I use fairly shallow dadoes in case joinery — $\frac{1}{8}$" to $\frac{3}{16}$", occasionally as much as $\frac{1}{4}$". The former cuts are within the router's one-pass capability, the latter depth is stretching it.

If you need a $\frac{3}{8}$" or deeper dado for something, you'll have to do it in more than one pass. To get the full depth, you can adjust the bit extension between passes, or you can use shims between the sled bottom and the workpiece for the first pass, remove them for the second.

While a saw-powered dado cutter hogs away dadoes quickly, remember that the router has pluses to compensate for its lower cutting speed. The primary one is that you can size the cut easily. Another plus is that the cut is invariably clean and square — no raggedy bottom.

Dado large workpieces on a router table with a sled like a table-saw crosscut sled. A stop clamped to the sled's fence locates the cut and immobilizes the work. Slides on the underside reference the edges of the tabletop to guide the sled.

A stopped or blind dado (inset) is easy enough to cut on the router table. Mark the ends of the cut on the work, and the tangents of the bit on tape applied to the fence. Tip up the work so it is clear of the bit, line up the marks and begin the cut by plunging the work onto the cutter. If necessary, tip the work up off the bit to end the cut.

Stopped and Blind Cuts

What about stopped and blind cuts? Can you make them on the router table?

If a workpiece is of a manageable size, and if you can establish exactly where the bit is in relation to the work and the desired beginning and ending points, stopped grooves or dadoes you can cut easily enough. You lower the work onto the spinning bit to start the cut, or lift it off the bit to end the cut. In the case of the blind cut, you do both.

To know where to begin and end a stopped cut, mark the outer edges of the bit on a piece of tape stuck on the fence or the mounting plate.

To cut, line up the mark for the beginning of the groove with the mark on the fence to the left of the bit. Now drop the stock onto the bit, beginning the cut, and feed the work to the left. As the end-of-cut mark on the stock approaches to the mark on the fence to the right of the bit, carefully lift the end of the workpiece off the bit.

Obviously, if the workpiece is too big or unwieldy, you are going to have trouble maneuvering it. Also, if you're cutting the dado with the help of the dadoing sled, you'll have the same problem you had on the table saw — where, exactly, is the bit underneath the work?

With a Handheld Router

The router as a handheld tool remains a prime choice for dadoing large workpieces such as sides for a tall bookcase or base cabinet. It seems easier and safer to move a relatively small tool on a cumbersome workpiece than the other way around.

The big question is how you will guide the router for the cut, because, of course, it does need to be guided. You can use an edge guide if the cut is close to an edge. Even a straight board works

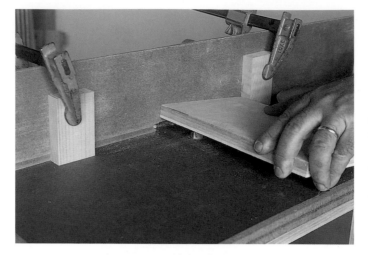

In a production mode — where you are repeating the same stopped or blind dado again and again — stop blocks clamped to the fence eliminate the need to lay out each cut, and they ensure you'll begin and end each cut in the right places.

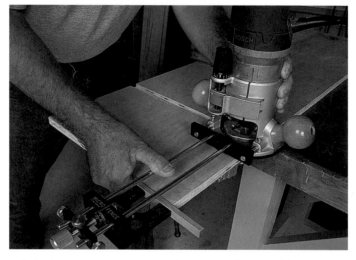

A dado (or groove) close to an edge is cut with a portable router equipped with an edge guide. Be wary of overextending the accessory, however. The farther apart the guide and the router, the greater the guide's tendency to "walk" along the edge. Keep a hand on the guide as well as the router throughout the cut.

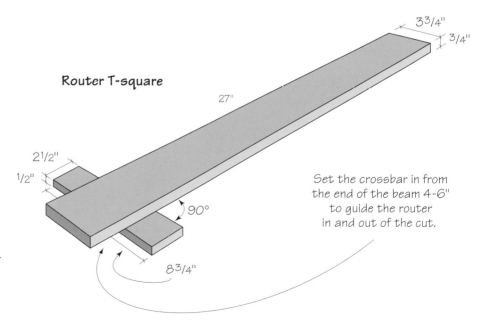

Router T-square

3³/4"
3/4"
27"
2¹/2"
1/2"
90°
8³/4"

Set the crossbar in from the end of the beam 4-6" to guide the router in and out of the cut.

as a guide. Measure from the desired cut location and position your fence. Align it with a try square and clamp both ends to the workpiece. Feed the router left to right along the fence (or, to put it another way, counterclockwise).

You can use a manufactured straight-edge clamp like the Tru-Grip. While separate clamps aren't needed with such a device, you still need to align it with a square because it won't square itself to an edge. You have to check the alignment with an accurate square.

A shop-made T-square, accurately assembled, is a great dadoing guide. It will square itself, and all you have to do is clamp it.

A setup gauge is helpful here. Cut a scrap to match the distance between the edge of the router base plate and the near cutting edge of the bit. Align one edge of the gauge to the shoulder of the desired cut and locate the T-square (or other guide) against the opposite edge. Bingo: The guide is set.

A crossbar attached at right angles to a plywood straightedge makes an easy-to-align T-square guide for dadoing with a router. Clamp it securely to the work and the bench top at each end.

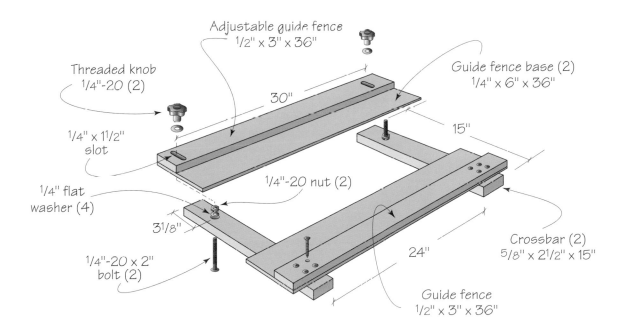

Threaded knob
1/4"-20 (2)

1/4" x 11/2"
slot

1/4" flat
washer (4)

Adjustable guide fence
1/2" x 3" x 36"

30"

Guide fence base (2)
1/4" x 6" x 36"

15"

1/4"-20 nut (2)

31/8"

1/4"-20 x 2"
bolt (2)

24"

Crossbar (2)
5/8" x 21/2" x 15"

Guide fence
1/2" x 3" x 36"

**Adjustable-width
dadoing jig**

Though more elaborate to construct, my favorite dadoing jig is easy to position on simple layout marks. It squares itself to the reference edge and adjusts easily to the exact width of dado you need. Size it to suit yourself; the drawing shows a jig scaled to accommodate 24"-wide (or less) workpieces.

The jig has two ½" plywood fences, each laminated to a ¼" plywood or MDF base strip. Both are matched to a particular router and bit by running that router along the fence, trimming the thin base with the bit. (Thereafter, that's the only router and bit combination you use with the jig.) One fence is then screwed to two hardwood crossbars. The bars must be perpendicular to the fence, of course. The second fence is mounted so it can be adjusted toward or away from the fixed fence (See illustration on page 24.)

Obviously, you can't produce a dado narrower than the cutting diameter of the bit, but you can easily make a wider one. Because the router is trapped between two fences, feed direction is less of an issue and miscuts are unlikely.

The bases make it easy to adjust the cut width and to position the jig on simple layout marks. To adjust the cut width, use a scrap or two of the stock to be housed in the cut as gauges. Set them against the fixed-fence base, slide the adjustable fence into position and lock it down. To position the jig, align the fixed-fence directly on one of the marks, with a crossbar tight against the work's edge. Secure the jig to the work with two clamps.

In making a guide for dadoing, keep in mind that the jigs don't have to be beautiful. Adjustability may seem desirable, but that's often where imprecision creeps in. Keep it as simple as possible.

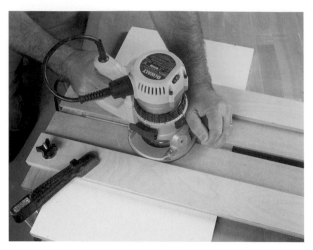

With the adjustable-width dadoing guide, cutting a dado is foolproof. The router is trapped between fences and can't veer off course, regardless of your feed direction. Reference the left fence as you push the router away; reference the right one as you pull it back, completing the cut.

Set the fence base edge directly on your layout line to position the jig. The crossbars ensure it will be perpendicular to the reference edge.

The gap between the fence bases represents the cut width. Pinch scraps of the work material between them to set up the jig. The cut you make will match their thickness perfectly.

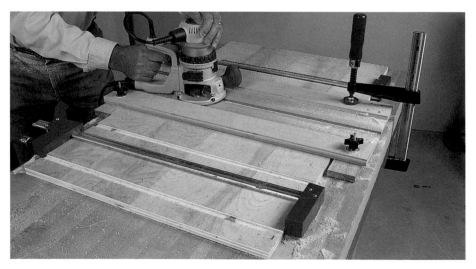

Dadoing bookshelf sides? Clamp them edge to edge and rout both at the same time.

Stopped Dadoes and Grooves

Any of these guides will work for through, stopped or blind cuts. You can mark starting and/or stopping points on the work itself or, for multiples, attach a stop or two to the guide.

In terms of choosing the best approach for making a stopped/blind cut, the hand-guided router is my instinctive choice for a dadoing casework. With the router on top of the work, you can see your layout marks, and you can see the cut as it is formed.

While I favor fixed base routers for hand-guided cuts like dadoes and grooves, stopped and blind cuts are the stuff of plunge routers. With a plunger, you can jab the bit into the work to start your cut, then quickly retract it at the end.

But that doesn't mean you have to have or use a plunge router for these cuts. Obviously, ending a stopped cut is easy, even with a fixed-base router. Just stop cutting at the mark, turn off the router and, when the bit stops spinning, lift it from the work.

While it takes a little practice to master, it isn't difficult to tip in or drag in the bit with a fixed-base router to start a cut. Align the cutter with the start mark. Rear the router back so its base plate, though not flat on the work, nevertheless is in contact with both the fence and the work. Turn on the router and carefully, slowly lower the spinning bit into the work. Practice. You want the axis of the bit aligned with the dado, so you don't create a bulb where the bit enters the work.

Screw a stop to a T-square if you need to produce identical stopped dadoes in a stack of casework parts. Move the T-square from one part to another and the stop moves too.

For stopped or blind dadoes, clamp stop blocks to the adjustable width jig (rather than the work). Move the jig, and the stops move with it. Using the plunge base eases beginning and ending these cuts.

With a little practice, you can master "tipping in" the bit, which allows you to make blind cuts with a fixed-base router. Tip the leading edge of the router's base onto the work and bring it against the guide fence. In one motion, lower the bit into the work and begin advancing the router along the fence.

RABBET JOINTS

The rabbet joint surely is one of the first joints tackled by newbie woodworkers. The rabbet is pretty easy to cut, it helps locate the parts during assembly, and it provides more of a mechanical connection than does a butt joint.

Back when I was tackling my first home improvement projects, I remember thinking that with practice I'd "outgrow" rabbet joints. Of course, I'm still cutting rabbets because woodworkers never "outgrow" them.

Rabbet Joinery

The most common form is what I call the single-rabbet joint. Only one of the mating parts is rabbeted. The cut is proportioned so its width matches the thickness of the mating board, yielding a flush fit.

For this joint, the depth of the rabbet should be one-half to two-thirds its width. When assembled, the rabbet conceals the end grain of the mating board. The deeper the rabbet, the less end grain exposed in the assembled joint.

In the double-rabbet joint, both the mating pieces are rabbeted. The rabbets don't have to be the same but typically they are.

The rabbet works as a case joint and as an edge joint. Case joints generally involve end grain, while edge joints involve only long grain. In casework, you often see rabbets used where the top and/or bottom join the sides (end grain to end grain), and where the back joins the assembled case (both end to end and end to long). In drawers, it's often used to join the front and sides.

Because end grain glues poorly, rabbet joints that involve it usually are fastened either with brads or finish nails, or with screws concealed under plugs. (Don't sweat the concealment in utilitarian constructions.)

Woodworkers don't necessarily think of the rabbet as an edge-to-edge joint, yet they all know of the shiplap joint. Rabbet the edges of the mating boards and nest them together. Voila!

It's also a great right-angle edge join, as seen in the case-side-and-back combination and also in practical box-section constructions such as hollow legs and pedestals. Long grain joins long grain in these structures. Since it glues well, the result is a terrific, strong joint.

You can gussy up the joint's appearance by chamfering the edge of the rab-

Rabbet joints

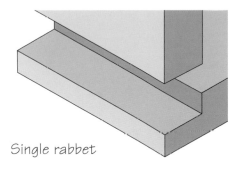
Single rabbet

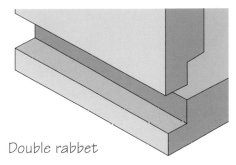
Double rabbet

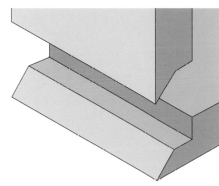
Mitered rabbet

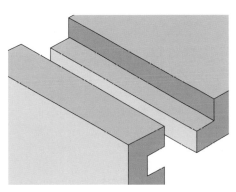
Dado and rabbet

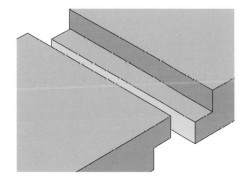
Shiplap

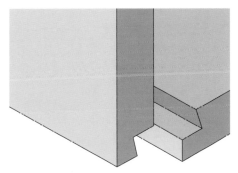
Dovetail rabbet

Cutting rabbets on the table saw requires a series of setup steps — each is accomplished in a matter of minutes — beginning with the shoulder cut. With the fence out of the way, adjust the blade height. I use a gauge block, but you can use a rule or some other gauge.

bet. When the joint is assembled, the chamfer separates the face grain of one part from the edge grain of the other. Since the chamfer is at an angle to both faces, it won't look inappropriate even though its grain pattern is different.

One variant worth spotlighting is the rabbet-and-dado joint. This is a good rack-resistant joint that assembles easily because both boards are positively located. The dado or groove doesn't have to be big; often it's a single saw kerf, no deeper than one-third the board's thickness. An offset tongue, created on the mating board by the rabbet, fits into it.

It's a good choice for plywood casework, because it's often difficult to scale a dado or groove to the inexact thickness of plywood. It's far easier to customize the width of a rabbet. So you cut a stock-width dado, then cut the mating rabbet to a custom dimension. An extra cutting operation is required, but the benefit — a big one — is a tight joint.

There are lots of good ways to cut rabbets. The table saw, jointer and router all come to mind. The most versatile techniques center around the table saw and the router.

Rabbeting on the Table Saw

The table saw offers at least two different ways to make rabbets. The method you choose is influenced by the number of rabbets you have to cut, as well as the sizes and proportions of the workpieces.

It's quickest to cut the rabbets using whatever blade is in the saw. Two passes are all it takes. But if you have lots of rabbets to cut or if the workpieces are too big to stand on edge safely (or comfortably), it's best to use a dado cutter. (A dado cutter is especially appropriate if your job entails dadoes as well as rabbets.)

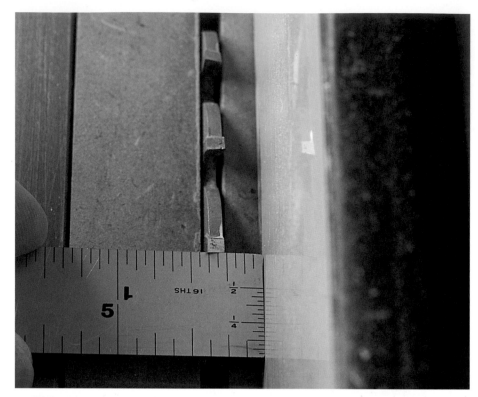

The fence can be positioned using a rule (top) or a scrap of the stock that will be housed in the rabbet (above). The only trick is to be sure you measure from the outside of the blade. The fence's scale won't work for this setup.

Make the shoulder cut, using the fence as a guide. Keep the workpiece tight against the fence and apply pressure as well to keep it flat on the saw table. A (consumable) pusher placed over the line of the cut does the latter.

SAW-BLADE RABBETING

The quick method: I use whatever blade is in the saw — usually a general-purpose blade. (The approach isn't quick if you start by changing table-saw blades!)

It's a good idea to use a zero-clearance throat plate. On the second cut, the workpiece will be standing on edge, and you'll feed it between the fence and the blade. You don't want the work to get hung up on the throat plate.

The first cut you make forms the shoulder. To set up, adjust the blade height for the depth of the rabbet. There are a variety of setup tools you can use, but it's always a good idea to make a test cut so you can measure the actual depth of the kerf.

That done, position the fence to locate the rabbet's shoulder. Doing so establishes the rabbet width, so measure from the face of the fence to the outside of the blade.

The cutting procedure is to lay the work flat on the saw table, then run the edge along the fence and make the shoulder cut. If you are rabbeting the long edge of a board, use just the fence as the guide. When cutting a rabbet across the end of a piece, guide the work with your miter gauge and use the fence simply as a positioning device. It is easy to set up, and the miter gauge keeps the work from "walking" as it slides along the fence. Because no waste will be left between the blade and the fence, you can do this safely.

Nevertheless, if you feel uneasy about using the miter gauge and fence together, use a stand-off block. Clamp a scrap (your stand-off block) to the fence near the front edge of the saw table. Be sure you move the fence away from the blade to account for the block's thickness. Lay the work in the miter gauge and slide it against the scrap. As you make the cut, the work is clear of the fence.

Having cut the shoulders of all the rabbets, you next adjust the setup for the bottom cut. You may need to change the height of the blade, the fence position, or both.

Adjust the blade elevation to match the width of the rabbet. You can use one of your test pieces to gauge this adjustment, then reposition the fence. To avoid having the waste fire back at you, make sure it will fall to the outside of the blade. Thus, the gap between blade and fence equals the stock thickness remaining after the rabbet is complete.

As I said, this bottom cut is made with the workpiece standing on edge, its kerfed face away from the fence. Bear in mind that this cut can be pre-

In most instances the blade is readjusted to make the bottom cut. A rule will work, but a shoulder-cut sample is the most accurate gauge. Raise the blade so its teeth just skim the shoulder; you don't want a ridge of waste where the shoulder meets the bottom.

For the bottom cut, the work must stand on edge: a balancing act for a very large workpiece. The ledge formed by the cut passes between the fence and the blade, the waste falls to the outside.

carious if the workpiece is big. You can help steady the work with a featherboard pressing the work against the fence. Or you can mount a tall facing to the fence.

But for me, these "extra" tasks push the approach out of the quick realm. If the workpiece is too large to perch on edge and feed along the rip fence comfortably, I'll try another approach. If it's a one-off rabbet, I generally reach for a router. If it's one of many rabbets, I may take a deep breath, unplug the saw, and get out the dado cutter.

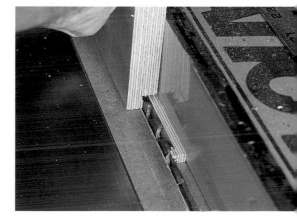

Conventional woodworking wisdom stipulates that you avoid leaving the waste from a cut between the blade and the fence, so what you see here violates the rule. But a tiny sliver — the waste produced when cutting a $\frac{3}{8}$" x $\frac{3}{8}$" rabbet with a saw blade — isn't a hazard in my experience.

DADO-CUTTER RABBETING

Rabbeting on the table saw with a dado cutter has a variety of advantages.

• You can keep the work flat on the saw table.

• The rabbet is cut in one pass. No need to change setups for the shoulder but and bottom cut. No staged cuts to nibble off the waste.

• One setup completes the job.

Where the proportions of the workpiece allow it, use the rip fence to guide the cut. Don't fret about the width of the dado stack so long as it exceeds the width of the rabbet you want. Clamp a sacrificial facing to the fence and bury the cutter in this facing.

The sacrificial facing should be, at minimum, $\frac{1}{2}$" thick ($\frac{3}{4}$" is better). Use something flat (plywood, MDF, melamine). The work is going to be flat on the saw table, so you can use a pair of clamps to secure the facing. Locate them out of the feed path.

With the facing in place, lower the cutter and position the fence so the facing (but not the fence itself) is over the cutter. Turn on the saw and raise the cutter about $\frac{3}{8}$" to $\frac{1}{2}$". This done, you'll be able to bury the cutter in the fence, exposing only the width you need for the rabbet you are cutting. It's very easy to set the exact cut width because you only have to move the fence; you don't have to fiddle with shims and chippers in the dado stack.

Making a cut is a straightforward matter of sliding the workpiece along the fence and across the cutter. As long as your workpiece is flat, your feed rate is appropriate and you apply some down force on the work as you feed it, you should end up with a clean, accurate rabbet.

If the workpiece proportions aren't suited to being guided along the fence, add the miter gauge to the setup. Everything else remains as I've described it — a fence with sacrificial facing and dado cutter partially buried in the fence. Simply advance the work,

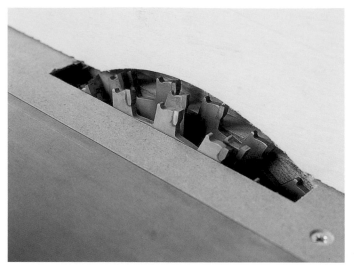

A dado stack set is excellent for cutting rabbets. Rather than struggle with adjusting it to a precise cut width, set it up for its maximum. Then clamp a strip of plywood (or like material) to the rip fence. Set the fence so the plywood is over the cutter, and raise the cutter to produce a fingernail cut into the plywood (but not the fence).

Cutting a rabbet with the dado head isn't significantly different from ripping or dadoing a panel on the table saw. Apply just enough pressure with your left hand to keep the workpiece square against the fence as you feed it along the fence and across the cutter (above). The cutter hogs out the rabbet (left) in a single pass.

its end butted against the fence, through the cut with the miter gauge.

Alternatively, you can use a crosscut sled to support the work and guide the cut. You get the same advantages in rabbeting that you do with dadoing: The work doesn't move, the box does. Obviously, you don't use the rip fence. But you can still use an over wide dado cutter. Clamp a stop block to the cut-off-box fence to position the work to yield the width of rabbet you want.

Jointer-Cut Rabbets

The jointer will make quick work of rabbets you need to cut along the grain. Most have what's called a rabbeting ledge to the left of the cutterhead. To use it, you lower the infeed table to the width of the rabbet desired and bring the fence into position to control the depth of the rabbet (and support the work).

As long as the work stands on edge (or end), face against the fence, you will leave the guard in place for the operation. It shrouds the corner of the cutter that produces the rabbet. Contemporary jointers have guarding behind the fence to cover the cutterhead during this sort of operation. But on older models, moving the fence across the jointer tables exposes the cutterhead. If you have an older jointer, I recommend that you DON'T use it for rabbeting.

A jointer has plenty of power, so one pass will cut just about any rabbet regardless of width or depth. Pace your feed rate to get a clean cut and avoid chipping or splintering.

While the jointer is terrific for rabbets running along the grain, it is problematic for cross-grain rabbets. Here's why:

• Unless your knives are really sharp, the cut quality won't be as good as a saw or router cut.

• Workpiece orientation becomes an issue. If you stand the work on end, you can leave the guard in place, which is

Rabbeting the end of a long, narrow workpiece calls for the aid of a miter gauge. The fence still limits the width of cut, but the miter gauge guides the movement of the workpiece.

A crosscut sled is a great accessory for rabbeting with a dado head on the table saw. The work is immobilized — yes, the sled moves, but the work is stationary on the sled — so you don't have to worry about your panel twisting or "walking" as you feed it through the cut. But a stop block is essential to set the width of cut. Measure from the outside of the stack and butt your stop against the rule end (left). Then clamp the stop to the sled fence.

good. But a tall workpiece on end may be difficult to control throughout the cut. The alternative — guard removed and workpiece end cantilevered off the rabbeting ledge — is unacceptable.

A second limitation of the rabbeting jointer is its steel knives. Unless you like sharpening them, you won't use the jointer for rabbeting plywood, particleboard or other glue-laden materials.

The upshot for me is that I limit my jointer rabbeting to long-grain cuts in solid wood. It's great for shiplap joints, for example.

Even large rabbets are cut in a single pass on the jointer. The work ideally should be on edge, its face flat against the fence. This allows you to use the guard and offers the best support for the workpiece.

To set up the jointer for a rabbet, slide the fence across the table. Measure from the corner of the knife to the fence to establish the shoulder depth. Note that on this jointer model, the fence support mechanism shields the bulk of the cutterhead. Then lower the infeed table to establish the width of the rabbet.

Rabbeting with the Router

The router is an excellent tool for rabbeting, in part because you can deploy it as a hand tool. For some jobs, you just want to immobilize the workpiece and move the cutting tool over it. In those situations, the router is the tool to use.

Occasionally, you may want to cut a rabbet into an assembly — perhaps a frame for a door or lid. If you use a router, you can wait until the frame is glued up and sanded, then produce the rabbet for a pane of glass or a panel. You do have to square the inside corners, but that's a simple process with a chisel.

A major benefit of the handheld router approach is that you can see the cut as it is formed. On the table saw (and the router table as well), the work itself conceals the cut.

You can cut rabbets on the router table as well, of course. The operation is similar to rabbeting on the table saw with a dado head. But I want to focus primarily on handheld approaches.

A rabbeting bit is the commonly used cutter, but it is not the only one that will work. If you use an edge guide to control the cut, you can use a straight bit or a mortising bit.

The rabbeting bit is piloted, and the typical bit makes a $\frac{3}{8}$"-wide cut. Most manufacturers set rabbeting sets, which bundle a stack of bearings with the cutter. Want to reduce the cut width? Switch to a larger bearing. The set I have yields six different widths from $\frac{1}{2}$" to $\frac{1}{8}$" (no $\frac{3}{16}$" available, for some reason). With the largest bearing, the bit can handle flush trimming work. More extensive sets are available, of course.

The piloted bit enables you to rabbet curved edges (can't do that on the table saw). Making a cut with a piloted rabbeting bit is pretty much a matter of setting the cut depth, switching on the router and diving in. Cut across the grain first, then with the grain. If you are routing only across the grain, either climb-cut in from the corner or clamp a backup scrap at the corner to prevent blowout as the bit exits the work.

The bit and the bearings work very well, but I'm often inclined to use an unpiloted bit with an edge guide for rabbeting. I get an infinitely variable cut width with this setup, rather than a few predetermined widths. In addition, I have better control of the tool and the cut.

With a piloted bit alone, the cutting edges begin their work before the bearing makes contact with the edge. All too often, a dip occurs around the corner of the workpiece at one end of the cut or the other. This doesn't happen with an edge-guide controlled cut, because the guide surface extends well beyond the cutter both before and after. Keep the guide in contact with the workpiece edge throughout the feed — beginning before the cut actually starts and continuing until the bit is clear of the work — and you won't have trouble.

The latter is especially true if you elect to circumvent a blowout by climb-cutting in from a corner. The guide gives you that good control.

STOPPED AND BLIND RABBETS

A rabbet doesn't have to extend the full length of an edge. It can terminate shy of one end (a stopped rabbet) or shy of both ends (a blind rabbet).

These cuts are tough to do on the table saw or jointer but easy to make with a router or on the router table. The most simple approach is to put a mark at the two ends of the rabbet you want to cut. With a handheld router, you visually align the bit with the start mark as you begin cutting and stop when the you reach the end mark.

Of course, you must be able to see the marks, and you need to begin and end right at the marks.

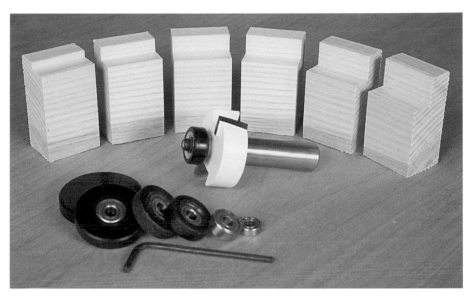

One rabbeting bit with an assortment of bearings enables you to rout rabbets of different widths. The eight bearings in this older set produce seven rabbet widths and a flush-trimming capability. Sets are available with many more bearings if you have the cash to spend, the inclination to use them and the disposition to keep them organized.

First choice for many rabbeting cuts is a piloted rabbeting bit installed in a portable router. Setup is minimized — chuck the bit in the router, set the cut depth and rout. You can use the portable router on the largest work, even on already assembled projects.

An edge guide is a big help here. To use one, you brace the tip of the guide against the workpiece edge, shift the whole router as necessary to align the bit for the start of the cut, then pivot the router into the cut.

On the router table, you must, in addition to marking the workpiece, place marks on the router-table fence that correspond to the bit edges. To make a stopped cut, line up the workpiece against the fence, then pull the leading end away so it bypasses the bit. Align the start mark on the work beside the bit mark on the outfeed side. Push the work against the fence (and, thus, onto the bit), feed through the cut and, as the end mark comes into line with the bit mark on the infeed side, pull the work away from the fence.

An alternative approach on the router table is to use stop blocks, especially for a job in which you are producing a stack of identical workpieces. Simply clamp the blocks to the fence and layout is almost completely eliminated.

The starting block will be to the right, the stop block on the left. The quickest, easiest way to do it is to lay out the extents of the cut on a work sample, then do a dry run. Align the sample for the start of the cut and position the starting block against the trailing end of the piece. Move to the end point and position the stopping block against the leading end of the piece.

Obviously, the length of your fence can pretty easily be outstripped. When this happens, either attach a temporary facing that's long enough for the task at hand or skip the stops and use the visual alignment method.

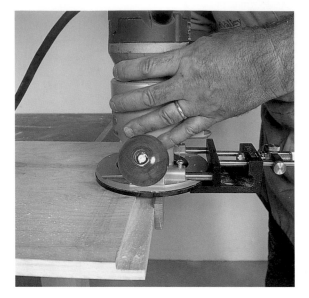

With an edge guide on your router, you can use a straight bit or a mortising bit to produce custom-width rabbets, including those that outstrip the width capacity of any rabbeting bit. In addition, the edge guide gives you better control of the operation than a pilot bearing, especially at the beginning and end.

On the router table, you can use a rabbeting bit but you have a lot more flexibility in terms of cut width if you use a mortising bit (a.k.a. planer bit or bottom-cleaning bit) instead. Regardless of the bit, you should use the fence for a straight cut. The pilot-free bit eliminates interference from the pilot on extra-wide cuts.

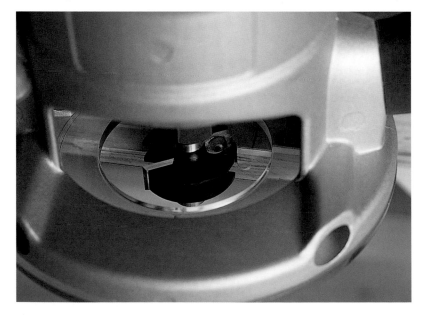

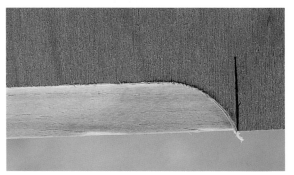

Stopped and blind cuts are simple and sure with a handheld router. Mark where you want the cut to begin and end, then rout. Rest the base on the work with the bit clear of the edge, then pivot into the cut. It's easy to watch the cut progress through the base opening and swing the bit out of the cut at the ending mark. The rabbet will terminate in an arc (inset), but that's easy to square with a chisel.

MITER JOINTS

What joint would you use at the corners of a case or a frame?

From the standpoint of appearance, the miter joint should be at the top of your list. The only surfaces visible on a miter joint are the attractive ones, the faces and the edges. No matter how thin it is, that strip of exposed end grain — the butt of the board — is unattractive.

So you see the miter joint used for picture frames, architectural trim and furnituremaking, for assembling mouldings and occasionally in face and door frames. If you are making a small chest and you have a wide, long board with a killer figure, you can wrap that figure around the corners — without interruption.

The two forms of the joint — case or edge miters and frame or flat miters — are basically the same, though the fundamental cut differs. The case miter is formed by joining two beveled edges. The frame miter is formed by joining two pieces that have been mitered.

The miter joint is difficult in subtle ways and can be problematic. Structurally, it's pretty weak. Because it mates one tangentially cut end grain surface to another, it glues poorly. That's better than end grain to end grain, but not much. Run some fasteners into a miter joint, and you're driving them into end grain, where they won't hold very well. Angling them helps some, but again, not a lot.

A miter (or a bevel) is tough to cut accurately. As a result, you'll struggle with the assembly. The joints won't close because some of the cuts are about half a degree out.

Gluing and clamping the parts of a miter joint often is an exercise in torment and despair. There's no mechanical interlock to hold them in alignment, and glue just lubricates the natural tendency of the surfaces to creep. The trick is to find a way to prevent the mating pieces from sliding out of line when you apply clamping pressure.

Simple solutions to these and other difficulties exist, and the results make it a joint worth mastering.

Positioning rip fence for bevel cuts

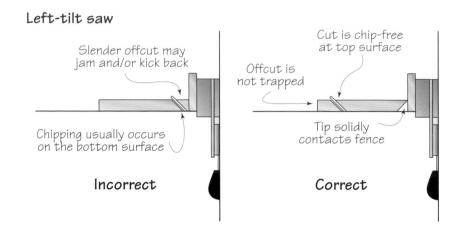

Left-tilt saw

Slender offcut may
jam and/or kick back

Cut is chip-free
at top surface

Offcut is
not trapped

Chipping usually occurs
on the bottom surface

Tip solidly
contacts fence

Incorrect   **Correct**

Right-tilt saw

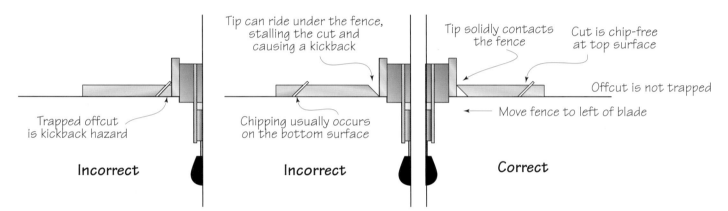

Tip can ride under the fence,
stalling the cut and
causing a kickback

Tip solidly contacts
the fence

Cut is chip-free
at top surface

Offcut is not trapped

Trapped offcut
is kickback hazard

Chipping usually occurs
on the bottom surface

Move fence to left of blade

Incorrect   **Incorrect**   **Correct**

Cutting Case Miters

Accurate 45° bevels on the mating parts are essential for the case miter. You can cut the bevels on a radial arm, compound miter or sliding compound miter saw. The capacity of the latter two saws is limited, typically under 12 inches. All three have some accuracy shortcomings.

The likelihood is you'll cut the bevels on a table saw. Tilt the blade to 45° and, depending on the proportions of the workpiece, guide the work through the cut with the miter gauge or along the rip fence. All is well until you run into one (or more) of the problems lurking in the process.

Be wary, first of all, of kickback. If you are using the rip fence as the guide, always locate it so the sawblade tilts away from it. With the blade tilted toward the fence, the offcut trapped between the blade and the fence can't lift off the table. It's all but certain it'll fire back toward you.

If you have a left-tilt saw, the customary fence location (to the right of the blade) is the correct, safe one for bevels. But most saws tilt toward the right so the fence will have to be moved to the left of the blade. In any event, be sure you stand to the left of the blade, out of Kickback Alley.

The most disheartening problem is the one that isn't evident until all the joints are cut and you start assembling them. The bevel angle is off a degree or two and the joints aren't square. Maybe you didn't tilt the blade enough, but more likely the fault is hiding in the adjustment and alignment of the saw.

You should know whether or not you can trust the scale on your saw when you tilt the blade for this cut. If you aren't absolutely certain it is accurate, use a drafting triangle to check the blade's angle. Crank the blade to its maximum height, tilt it, then check it. Make sure the triangle is flat against the plate, not against a carbide tip.

As a double-check, make a pair of test cuts and join the two samples. If the corner they form is square, your setup is right. Proceed with the workpieces.

Use a 45° drafting triangle to check the angle of the blade's tilt. Crank the blade as high as it will go, then tilt it. Make sure the triangle is against the plate and not registering on a carbide tip.

Make sure your miter gauge is square to the blade for a bevel cut. Use a drafting triangle to check the alignment before you tilt the blade.

You won't always use the rip fence. If the edge being beveled is the short one, you'll use the miter gauge. This common accessory is, of course, another source of inaccuracies. If you do use a miter gauge, square it to the blade with the drafting triangle before tilting the blade.

Instead of a miter gauge, a lot of people use a crosscut sled, specifically to ensure square cuts. The crosscut sled can be used for bevels too.

If you do a lot of bevel cuts and think it worth the materials and shop time, you can make a sled exclusively for bevel cuts. You'll derive a couple of benefits. One is the unmistakable angled kerf you can use to align the workpiece. Another is zero clearance around the kerf, which helps minimize chipping on the underside of the workpiece. If you work with veneered or melamine-coated sheets, this is a benefit you'll appreciate.

Finally, if you are using a contractor's saw, you may be reluctant to tilt the blade at all. Doing so often throws such saws out of alignment. Instead of tilting the blade, you can use an angle sled to deliver the work to the blade. The workpiece is tilted instead of the blade.

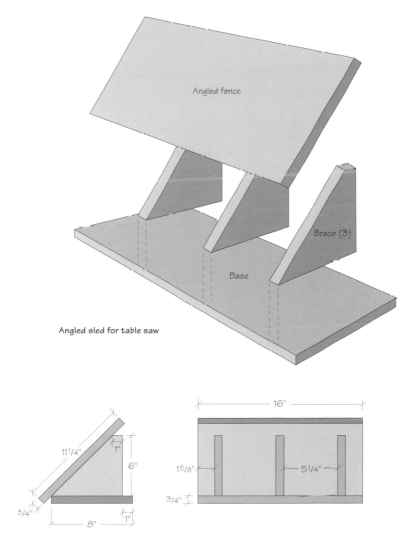

Angled sled for table saw

The angle sled is a simple device that enables you to saw bevels at whatever angle you build into the sled without tilting your table saw's blade. No bevel cuts are required to make the sled's parts, as the base and fence are square-edged. The braces are mitered. Use whatever flat panels you find in your scrap bin.

You can saw a bevel without tilting the table-saw blade if you use an angle sled to hold the workpiece. Rest the workpiece on the sled's angled fence, with its edge square on the table saw. Clamp it to the sled. Then feed the sled along the saw's rip fence to make the cut.

A backup strip attached to the miter gauge aids in locating the bevel cut. Align your layout line with the kerf in the strip.

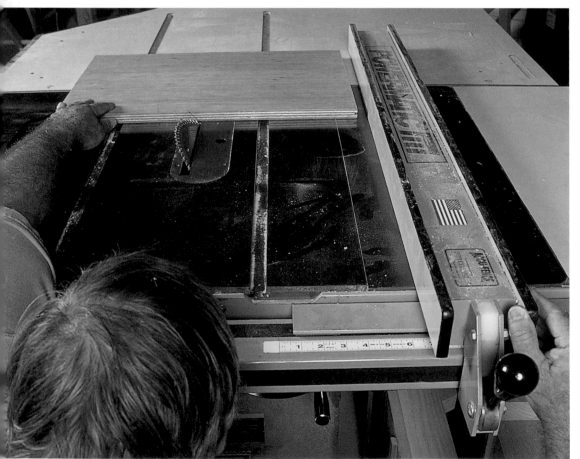

Aligning the work for the cut is less straightforward, perhaps, than you might think. If you are using the crosscut sled or a miter gauge with a backup strip, you have a kerf to use.

But there's no practical way to measure directly from the tilted blade to position the fence. Instead, you have to lay out the bevel cut on the stock and align the layout line with the blade. Then bring the fence into position. It's easy to do this with the stock on the outfeed side of the blade. Sight across the tilted blade to your layout line on the work's edge. Gently slide the fence against the work and lock it.

ROUTING A BEVEL

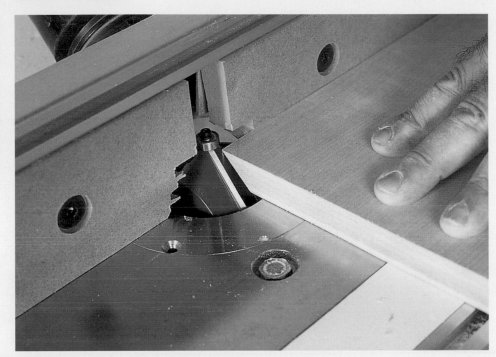

"Tune" rough-sawed bevels with a chamfering bit. To bevel the full edge of $\frac{3}{4}$" stock, you need a very large bit, so it's best to do this on a router table, with the router speed dialed back to about 12,000 rpm. You could produce the bevel from a square edge this way, but it's best to stage the cut. Bear in mind that routing cross-grain is tough on both cutter and router. The cut finish won't be great either, so limit this approach to long-grain cuts.

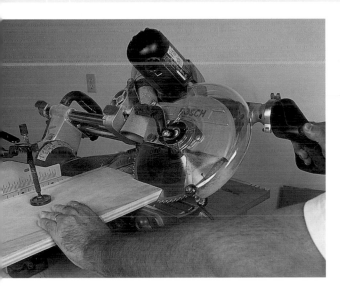

Bevels for boxes, bookcases and other constructions with relatively narrow parts are doable on a miter saw. A slider has the greatest crosscut capacity. Tilt the saw head for the cut.

For a bevel cut, always locate the rip fence so the saw blade tilts away from it. The fence won't trap the waste under the blade.

Cutting Frame Miters

Cutting miters seems simple. You can use any of several different power saws, from the table saw to the sliding compound miter saw, to make them. The trick is to cut a precise angle that yields a square joint.

Power miter saws and radial-arm saws have adjustment points that sometimes contribute inaccuracies. A detent has a tiny bit of play, the pointer on the scale may be off a hair and pivot points can develop play.

Nevertheless, these tools will produce acceptable results: It's routine for trim carpenters, who move briskly through new buildings, installing casing around windows and doors. They use miter saws to make the cuts, and the joints they produce typically are nice and tight. Repetition yields proficiency.

Having a well-tuned saw helps too. And when you make a critical cut, check the angle against a reliable angle square. For 45° angles, a plastic drafting triangle is both accurate and inexpensive.

A woodworker who gets little practice may get better results using a sliding crosscut table or a miter sled on the table saw. Sliding tables are pricey accessories, and not all saws will accommodate one. An adjustable miter sled is more reasonably priced — the Dubby is a familiar brand. Or you can make one.

The advantage of these devices over a miter gauge is that the work is immobilized against the fence and base throughout the cut. You aren't sliding the work itself across the saw table.

Presuming your goal is to produce a square corner, and not necessarily to produce precise, individual 45° cuts, you can make yourself a miter sled for the table saw that will produce it. Use a square-cornered block for the fence, and attach it to the base.

The result is a sled that helps you cut clean miters that form perfect right-angle joints. No fuss, no adjustments, no fine-tuning required.

A fixed miter sled for the table saw produces perfect right-angle joints. Stops clamped to the aluminum angle fence extensions ensure parts are properly sized.

With the sled, cut one-half of the joint on the left side of the blade, the other part on the right side. The miter cuts may not be perfect 45° angles, but as long as the sled's fence block is a perfect right angle, the miters cuts will come together at a perfect right angle.

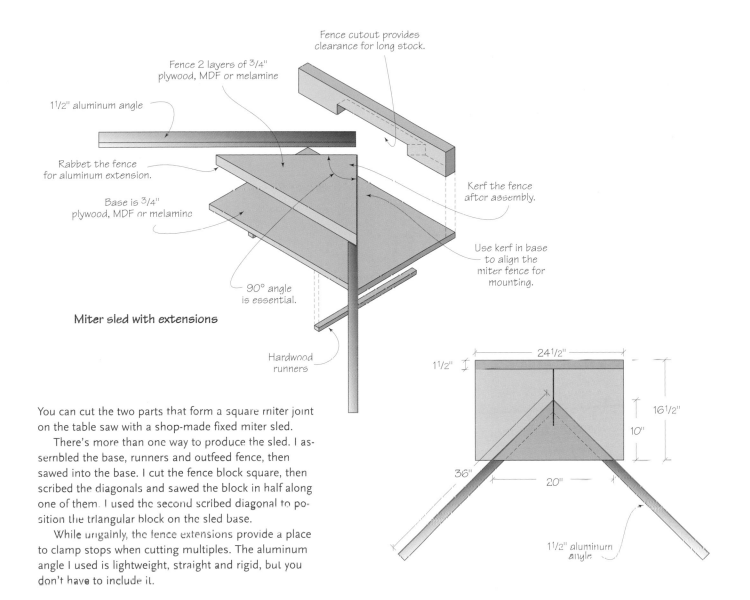

Fence cutout provides clearance for long stock.

Fence 2 layers of 3/4" plywood, MDF or melamine

1 1/2" aluminum angle

Rabbet the fence for aluminum extension.

Base is 3/4" plywood, MDF or melamine

Kerf the fence after assembly.

Use kerf in base to align the miter fence for mounting.

90° angle is essential.

Miter sled with extensions

Hardwood runners

24 1/2"

1 1/2"

16 1/2"

10"

36"

20"

1 1/2" aluminum angle

You can cut the two parts that form a square miter joint on the table saw with a shop-made fixed miter sled.

There's more than one way to produce the sled. I assembled the base, runners and outfeed fence, then sawed into the base. I cut the fence block square, then scribed the diagonals and sawed the block in half along one of them. I used the second scribed diagonal to position the triangular block on the sled base.

While ungainly, the fence extensions provide a place to clamp stops when cutting multiples. The aluminum angle I used is lightweight, straight and rigid, but you don't have to include it.

It's designed to cut miters, so why not use your miter saw? Pivot the saw table to the designed angle left or right, hold the work against the fence and make the cut. It's fast and easy when you're diligent about keeping the saw tuned. With both pivots and slides, the saw is susceptible to inaccuracies and large-diameter, thin-kerf blades are prone to deflect in heavy cuts.

Rip into narrow cauls for flat miters.

Sandpaper glued to back elimates slippage.

Leave wide for case miters.

Cut V groove across the wide board.

6" - 8"

3/4" - 1"

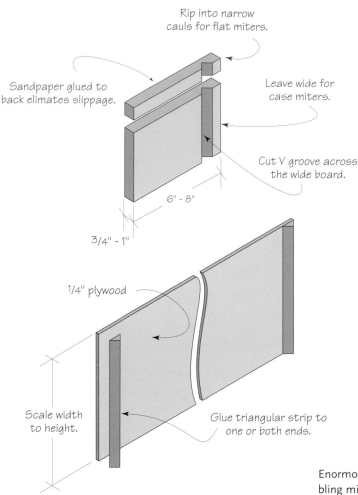

1/4" plywood

Scale width to height.

Glue triangular strip to one or both ends.

Miter clamping cauls

Assemble four joints at once with band clamps and V-grooved blocks at each corner. The blocks trap the tips of the joints, preventing them from moving out of alignment. Packing tape on the blocks prevents them from being glued to the assembly.

Enormously helpful in assembling miter joints, clamping cauls are easy to make. Here are just two approaches. Make a batch and store them with your clamps.

Assembling Miters

The challenge in gluing up miter joints is how to apply clamping pressure without forcing the joints out of alignment. You need to force the mating surfaces together, which requires pressure perpendicular to the glue line. You also need to pull the components of the assembly together.

You'll find all sorts of specialty clamps on the market. You can buy corner clamps, in a range of prices, for clamping individual miter joints. They'll work for both frames and open boxes (that is, boxes that have no top or bottom).

Some setups clamp a box or frame all at once. A band clamp, for example, surrounds the assembly and pulls its parts together. Corner blocks — use those supplied with the clamp, or make your own — simultaneously hold the parts together and distribute the clamp pressure.

If you are assembling a case, dealing with four corner blocks per band clamp can be difficult. To simplify clamping, make V-blocks scaled to the assembly and line them with packing tape to shed glue. The first band clamp holds them in place, and the remaining band clamps are easy to apply.

Glue tack will often hold a small box together while you position pressure blocks and apply clamps. Alternatively, you can use packing tape to hold the parts while you apply the clamps.

With a chest or cabinet, the parts are larger, more cumbersome, less cooperative. In these situations, it may be practical to address one joint at a time. Glue up two joints individually, then a half-hour later, after the glue has set, combine them into the box or case.

I personally favor some homebrewed approaches that use such general-purpose clamps as F-style and C-clamps.

Miter clamping cauls (see above illustration) provide angled surfaces so you can apply clamps perpendicular to the glue seam. Clamp the cauls to the mating parts, then close the joint and apply one or more clamps to it.

A sure way to assemble case miters is with shop-made miter clamping cauls. Clamp a caul to each half of the joint, then apply clamps to the joint. Do one joint at a time.

Miter clamping cauls help you apply clamping pressure at a right angle to the joint's seam. Align the cauls so the clamping pressure is concentrated on the middle of the joint, not at the tip or the inside corner.

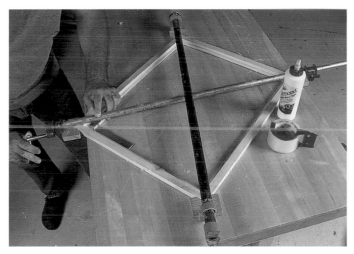

Packing tape holds glued miters together while you apply V-blocks and clamps. Apply bar or pipe clamps on the diagonals, and alternate tightening to avoid distorting the frame.

Screw V-blocks to a plywood base to make a frame clamping jig. Pressure is applied with pairs of wedges. Positioning the blocks — using frame parts — before gluing a frame, takes only a minute or two.

A second approach for clamping frames involves four notched clamping blocks. This works where you want to assemble four joints at once — a complete frame — as opposed to an individual joint.

You can use the blocks with a brace of bar clamps, applied diagonally. But positioning and tightening the clamps without distorting the frame is pretty tricky. On the few occasions I've done it this way, I secured each freshly glued joint with a wrap of packing tape.

Then I set the V-blocks at the frame corners and applied the bar clamps diagonally, alternating from clamp to clamp as I tightened them.

A better way to use the blocks is to mount them to a base. The base provides a flat surface to ensure the frame isn't twisted, and the V-blocks capture the frame corners to ensure they are square. It's particularly useful when you're making multiples, and for very large frames, where the support of the base is beneficial.

I set up the board after at least one frame is cut, so I can use its parts to position the blocks that are screwed to the base. Note that only two of the V-blocks are screwed to the base. The other two corners are fastened with cleats to the base. Twin wedges driven between the cleats and the loose V-blocks apply clamping pressure. To prevent squeeze-out from bonding the frame to the base or blocks, wax them liberally.

Keying Flat Miters

Miter joints can be reinforced in a number of ways. Picture framers commonly use nails. Splines or biscuits are pretty easy to incorporate, and you can hide them inside the joint.

Flat miters can be simultaneously reinforced and decorated with keys, either a spline or a dovetail. The required cut can be done on the table saw or router table. You assemble the frame, then set it in a carrier to make the cut. A key is glued in the cut, then trimmed flush.

Carrier construction is simple. Miter the ends of the two frame supports, then glue and screw them to the plywood or MDF back. The supports must be at right angles to each other. In this simple form, it can be used flat on the router table. If you use the jig upright, braced against the fence, add the fence hook to it.

The jig for slotting a frame can be oriented either of two ways — upright against the fence of either table saw or router table, or flat on the router table surface to cut with a slot cutter. For a dovetail slot, you can use any size or angle of dovetail bit. The 7° and 8° bits do give you slightly more cut depth than the 14° variety.

For a conventional straight cut, the table saw is the best choice. You can make a deep cut, which is important for frames with wide members.

On the router table, slot cutters are faster and give you a more usable selection of widths than straight bits. You can cut ½" deep in one pass; with a straight bit, you have to stage a deep cut. Slotters as thin as ¹⁄₁₆" are available. A narrow kerf allows you to double the splines, even in standard ¾" stock. Once you get below ¼", straight bits tend to be pretty frail.

However you orient the jig, the frame is set into it, and perhaps clamped with a spring clamp or two. Adjust the cutter height and the fence

Spline and dovetail keys are exposed splines. After the joint is glued up, you saw or rout a slot through its edge, then glue a key into the slot. Typically, the key is a contrasting wood.

Saw slots for spline keys in frames on the table saw. A shopmade jig holds the assembled frame. The jig straddles the rip fence.

Slots for dovetail keys are cut on the router table, using the same type of workholder. The slot can be centered easily by turning the frame around in the jig after the initial cut, then making a second pass.

position. Hold the jig and frame against the fence and make the cut. To center a cut, make two passes, flipping the frame over between them. You can use the same technique to cut a pair of slots — cut one slot in a joint, turn the frame over, then cut the second slot. Once the slots are cut, make keys to fit them.

Rip splines — contrasting wood is often used — to the appropriate thickness on the table saw. Plane them to fit; you want very tight glue lines. Crosscut the strips into little triangles and glue on into each slot. When the glue dries, trim them flush.

Cut dovetail keys on the router table. Right after slotting the frame, cut the keys using the same bit and same height setting. The only change in setup is to swing the fence over the bit, housing most of it. Start with an oversized in and methodically trim it to fit the slot. When you've got a good fit, rip the pin from the board. Then cut another pin and rip it from the board. Repeat the process until you have enough key stock. Next, cut the stock into short keys and glue a key into each slot.

Trim the keys flush after the glue dries. Saw the keys close to the surface. Trim the remaining stubs flush with a block plane — work from the corner in so you don't tear out splinters of the keys — or sand the stubs flush.

Cut the key strips parallel to the grain of the stock. Always work with the dovetail bit housed in the router-table fence, as here. Trapping the work between the fence and the bit can be dangerous.

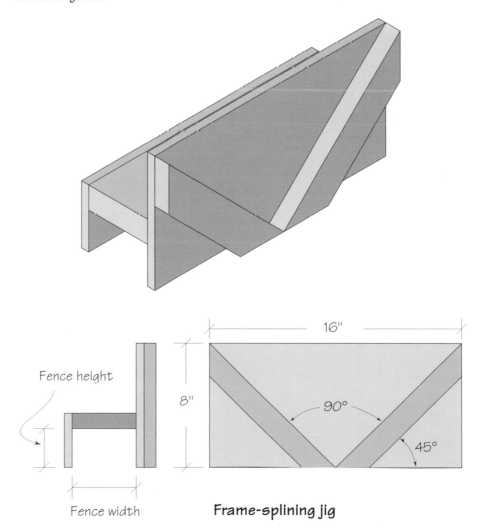

To slot picture frames and similar assemblies for keys, make this simple carrier. It holds a frame so you can cut through the corner on the table saw or router table. Even a huge frame can be worked in a carrier of this size.

Fence height

Fence width

16"

8"

90°

45°

Frame-splining jig

SPLINED JOINTS

Adding a spline to a joint sometimes increases the joint's strength and simplifies its assembly. It's an enhancement often advocated for edge joints but is most legitimate in a miter joint.

On the face of it, the process is simple. You cut grooves (or slots) in the mating surfaces of the joint. As you assemble the joint, you insert a spline, which bridges the seam and links the two pieces.

The hitch is that, in many splined joints, the spline's value is in the head of the builder rather than in the joint itself. Often the joint doesn't need it. For instance, edge-to-edge or edge-to-face butt joints, when well crafted, can hardly be made stronger.

But a spline is an excellent aid in assembling miter joints of all sorts. Note that the splines may be through, stopped or blind. In the former, the grooves for the spline are cut through from edge to edge and the ends of the spline are visible in the assembled joint. In the latter, the grooves end short of either edge and the spline is entirely concealed in the assembled joint. A stopped spline joint is the compromise: visible at one end, concealed at the other.

Spline Materials

The nature of the spline can have an impact on the method you use to cut the grooves. You can use solid wood or plywood for the splines.

Hardboard and MDF aren't good spline materials, in my opinion, because they have no grain. Without grain, these materials cannot reinforce a joint. You can view them as aligners, but they'll actually weaken the joint by reducing the good glue surface.

Plywood has several advantages and a couple of shortcomings, one of which I think is significant. It's strong because of its crisscrossing plies and it's stable for all practical purposes. That means you can saw up strips and glue them into the grooves without worries about grain orientation.

Appearance is sometimes an issue with plywood, so it's best limited to applications where one way or another it'll be concealed.

The significant reservation I have about plywood stems from its thickness. It's surprisingly difficult to cut a closely fitted groove for $\frac{1}{4}$" plywood, which isn't actually $\frac{1}{4}$".

At the table saw, two passes with the same setup gives you a centered groove for an edge-to-edge joint, and you can use the two cuts to customize the groove width. But grooving a face or a beveled edge with a standard blade takes you into two-setup territory. You need to adjust the fence position before making the second pass. A dado cutter might do, but the narrowest cut most will produce is $\frac{1}{4}$".

Thickness is an issue with a router too. You can buy a $\frac{7}{32}$" straight bit but the different $\frac{1}{4}$" plywoods are too thin for that width groove. (Metric bits are available; check them out when using imported plywood.)

You're probably wondering, how important is this? The fit is essential if your rationale for the spline is alignment. A $\frac{13}{64}$"-thick plywood spline in

two $\frac{1}{4}$"-wide grooves yields up to $\frac{3}{32}$" of misalignment. In addition, a spline fitted that poorly won't reinforce the joint either. Quite the contrary; it will weaken it.

Solid wood splines are extra work and demand extra savvy to orient. But you can customize the thickness to suit standard, easily cut groove widths: $\frac{1}{8}$", $\frac{3}{16}$" or even $\frac{1}{4}$". Moreover, if the spline is going to be visible, you can use either the working stock (so it nearly disappears) or a contrasting stock (as an accent).

The "savvy" part is that you must be reasonably wary of the spline's grain direction. The grain in the spline should parallel that in the mating parts. In a miter, the spline's grain should run perpendicular to the joint seam.

Clamp a small piece of $\frac{1}{4}$" hardboard in a vise and snap it off. Do the same with a hardwood ripping of the same thickness. When I did it, the hardboard broke pretty cleanly, right at the vise's jaws. The hardwood broke at the surface, then pulled some long fibers.

The groove is $\frac{1}{4}$" wide, but despite that dimension designation, the plywood isn't. This mismatch is unglueable. Look for a $\frac{7}{32}$" or a 5mm bit if you must use plywood for splines.

Orient the grain of a solid-wood spline perpendicularly to the glue line of the joint.

CUTTING THE GROOVES

The spline joints are so plentiful that it would be very repetitive to tell you, variation by variation, how to make them. The primary tools for cutting the grooves are, of course, the table saw and the router, either handheld or mounted in a table.

When you boil down all the variations, you discover that you have two basic cuts: into square edges and into beveled edges.

The setup steps are pretty routine for cutting square edges.

Select a cutter first. Using the table saw, ask yourself if a pass with the standard blade — one that typically produces a $\frac{1}{8}$" kerf — will be adequate. Can you make successive passes with a careful setup to produce a kerf width between $\frac{1}{8}$" and $\frac{1}{4}$"? Do you switch to the dado cutter, which has a minimum kerf width of $\frac{1}{4}$"?

At the router table, choose between the straight bit and the slot cutter. That done, select the cutter dimension.

The choice between straight or slot-cutter may come down to which you have. If you have both, workpiece orientation may enter into your decision. With a straight bit, the work is set on edge, face against the fence. With a slot-cutter, the work is flat on the tabletop.

If a centered groove is essential for some reason, you can cut it in two passes. But a centered groove seldom is essential. If you mark a reference face on each piece, grooving and assembly will proceed without a hitch. One-pass grooves save time.

Set the cutter and the fence. With the cutter selected and installed in the tool, the next step is to adjust the cutter's height. Then move the fence into position and lock it down.

Appropriate groove depths vary. In a square edge, you can cut $\frac{1}{2}$" or more deep. Limit a cut into the face to about one-third of the board thickness.

While a saw blade can cut to what-

There's no shortage of means available for cutting grooves for splines. Your table saw — equipped with its standard blade or a dado cutter — can breeze through most through cuts. A router, either portable or table-mounted, can be fitted with either a slot cutter or a straight bit to handle blind and stopped cuts.

The groove for a spline doesn't have to be centered on the stock. Setting up and actually cutting the grooves is completed more quickly if you allow the groove to fall where it may. But you do have to mark a reference face on each part, and make sure you consistently orient the face as you groove.

ever depth you chose, a straight router bit less than $\frac{1}{4}$" in diameter is prone to break if stressed too much. A $\frac{3}{8}$"- or $\frac{1}{2}$"-deep groove has to be cut incrementally, in bites of about $\frac{1}{8}$" to $\frac{3}{16}$". An alternative to raising the bit after each pass is to set the bit for the final cutting depth and use tabletop shims.

A slot cutter cuts through the fussy setups. Regardless of its cutting width, it'll cut to full depth in one pass without breaking. The cutter's elevation positions the groove. The depth of the groove is controlled by the fence.

In any case, position the fence, then "prove" the settings with a test cut. If you are making a two-pass cut, make both passes. Measure the cut itself, of course, then adjust the setup if necessary.

Mark a reference face on each workpiece. Unless you have the grooves dead on center, you'll want to ensure you are using the same face on each workpiece to index the cut. Otherwise, you'll create misaligned slots, defeating

your own purpose.

Make the cuts. Through cuts are straightforward, regardless of tool or tooling. The saw blade or slot cutter plows to full depth in a single pass. But if you're using a straight bit, it's best to do it in two or three passes.

Stopped and blind cuts should not be done on the table saw, as far as I'm concerned. It's easy to do them on the router table. Mark starting and stopping points on the fence. Align the end of the workpiece with the mark on the outfeed side, then plunge it onto the cutter. Feed right to left until the trailing end lines up with the mark on the infeed side. Then lift or pivot the work off the cutter.

Slotting the end of a workpiece is just as simple. A tall facing clamped to the router-table fence can support the work for a straight-bit cut. Use a large pusher to keep the workpiece square as you slide it along the fence.

If you are using a slot cutter, the work can rest flat on the tabletop.

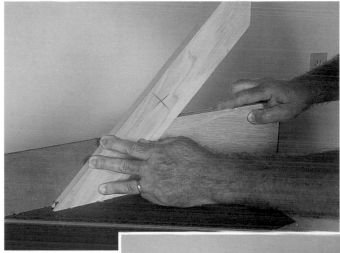

Long, narrow pieces are easier to control if you can rest them flat on the tabletop, rather than standing them on end. Using a slot cutter in a router table allows this. Use a scrap as a pusher to keep the piece square to the fence and to back up the cut.

Through cuts made in long edges, where you can slide the workpiece along the rip fence, are cut quickest on the table saw. Depth and stock hardness have little impact on feed rate. A cut-and-turn routine centers the groove in two passes.

That's a big benefit. You still need to use that pusher to help you move the workpiece in a controlled way and to back up the cut.

With either approach, it's a good idea to use a zero-clearance insert around the cutter. You definitely do not want the work to catch on an out-sized bit opening, whether in the fence or the tabletop. At best, it's a hiccup that's momentarily disconcerting. At worst, it can get the workpiece cocked and completely stall the feed.

On the table saw, you can use a tenoning jig to guide the cut. Here, too, use a zero-clearance insert so the end of the workpiece doesn't hang up on the too-generous opening common to the factory insert.

A flat miter is square edged, though you probably don't immediately think of it that way. The only difference I can think of between slotting a square-ended rail and slotting a flat miter is the cant of the workpiece. That angle will probably prevent you from securing it in a tenoning jig for slotting on the table saw. But you can mount a tall

Use an angled pusher to back up a through cut in a flat miter. A tall fence facing helps steady the work, and a zero-clearance auxiliary tabletop (a ⅛" hardboard covering) prevents the work from catching on an out-sized bit opening.

facing to your rip fence and use a pusher, just as you would on a router table.

With a flat miter, the pusher must be angled exactly like the miter. A workpiece will be leaning forward when you slot one end and leaning back when you slot the other. Use the same pusher for both cuts; simply roll it over between cuts.

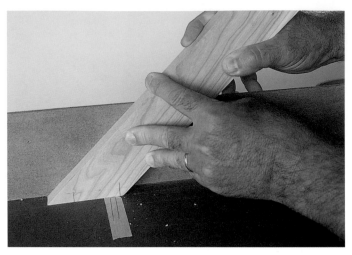

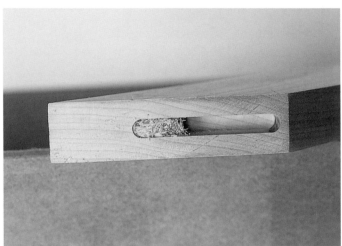

A stopped cut in a flat miter involves tipping the workpiece back, aligning it over the bit, then plunging and feeding to the stop mark. While a tall fence facing helps steady the work, a pusher always seems unnecessary. Lay out the extents of the slot on the workpiece's reference face. Align them with marks transferred onto the tabletop from the bit to control the length of the cut.

Grooving Bevels

The starting point for a successful splined miter joint, whether an edge miter or an end miter, is an accurate bevel on the stock. It doesn't matter if it's 45° for a right-angle joint or 30° or 22½° for six- or eight-sided assemblies.

The tilt of the saw blade must be accurately set, as must the fence position. Some saws tilt left, some right. To rip bevels, place the fence in such a way that the blade tilts away from it. This position allows you to make the cut without threat of the waste trapped between the blade and the fence, a kickback hazard. End bevels are cut either with a miter gauge or crosscut sled.

Edge bevels may be most accurately cut on the router table. Use a chamfering bit of the proper angle. But bear in mind that cross-grained cuts are taxing for the router and bit, and the cut quality will probably be marginal. So edge bevels, yes; end bevels, no.

With the workpieces beveled, lay out the spline groove on one piece. To avoid weakening the bevel tips, locate the spline slot very close to the joint's inside corner. No more than a ⅛" from it, I'd say. This placement simultaneously allows a ⅜"-deep cut without weakening the stock.

Decide how wide the slot will be, keeping in mind the tool you'll use to cut the slot. The spline doesn't need to

be very thick and, in most instances, a single saw kerf is satisfactory. If you want to make the spline thicker, you'll have to either use your dado cutter or kerf each piece, then reset the fence and widen the kerf on a second pass.

TABLE SAW APPROACHES

To slot an edge miter on the table saw, place the fence in such a way that the blade tilts away from it. Feed the stock along the fence with the sharp edge of the bevel against the fence. With an end miter, use the miter gauge to guide the stock. (The rip fence can safely be used to position the work for the cut. There's no offcut, and the fence will enable you to place each cut consistently.)

The particular table-saw approach I've just outlined will not work for everyone. I used a contractor's saw for two decades, and nearly every time I tilted the blade it threw the saw out of alignment. (You can bet I didn't do it often!)

The angle sled is a good jig that helps you cut the bevels and the spline grooves, both in edges and across ends. Clamp the workpiece to the sled and guide it along the saw's rip fence. The saw blade is perpendicular, but the work is tilted. With the work's face against the sled, cut the bevel. To cut the slots, turn the piece over so the bevel is against the saw table.

ROUTER TABLE APPROACHES

Working at the router table, you first must address what cutter you'll use, and how you'll handle the workpiece. Whatever cutter you use, you need a fence that's canted at the same angle as the edge miter. If you use a straight bit, the bevel must be flat on the tabletop. If you use a slot cutter, the bevel surface must be perpendicular to the tabletop.

Using a straight bit gives you a couple of options, while the slot cutter allows only one.

THE ACUTE-ANGLE FENCE

The simplest fence to make forms an acute angle with the tabletop. It's just a 4"- to 6"-wide length of 8/4 stock with a bevel ripped along one edge. Clamp it to the tabletop beside the bit, so the bevel forms an acute angle with the tabletop. You can make workable stopped and blind cuts with this fence, though their ends look a little weird. When the joint is assembled, the weirdness is your secret.

Beyond its simplicity, the acute-angle fence's advantage is that it traps the work, ensuring that the groove will appear where you want it to.

Slotting a bevel on the table saw is sure and safe. Place the rip fence where the blade tilts away from it. Ride the tip of the bevel along the fence to make the cut.

A shop-made angle sled allows you to cut both bevels and spline grooves on the table saw without tilting the blade. Clamp the work to the sled's sloping fence and guide the sled along the saw's rip fence to make the cut.

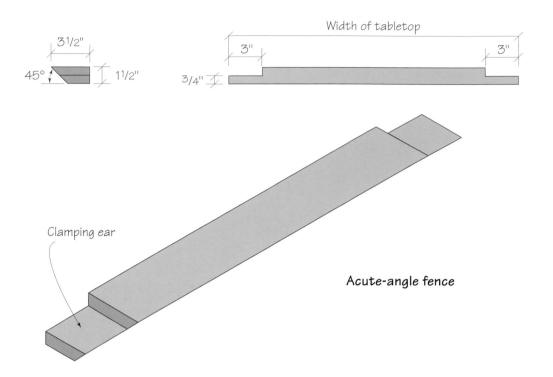

Clamping ear

Acute-angle fence

Make the acute-angle fence from a length of stock equal to the width of your router tabletop. Rip one edge of the fence with your table-saw blade tilted to 45°. (Obviously, if you are splining edge miters an angle other than 45° — the sides of a hexagonal or octagonal case, for example — the fence must be beveled at that angle.) At the band saw, cut the fence ends to form clamping ears.

Before setting up the acute-angle fence, adjust the bit height. Then, with one end of the fence clamped, use a workpiece with the spline groove laid out on it to align the fence. Sight along the fence to the bit and the workpiece just behind it. Swing the fence to line up the laid-out groove with the bit, then clamp the fence's free end.

Cutting through grooves is as simple as trapping the work in the crotch formed by the fence and the tabletop, then feeding it across the bit. As you do this, you want to keep some upward pressure on the workpiece's upper edge. An expendable push stick helps prevent tear-out, which often occurs when the bit exits the work. Make sure it fits tightly against the edge of the work.

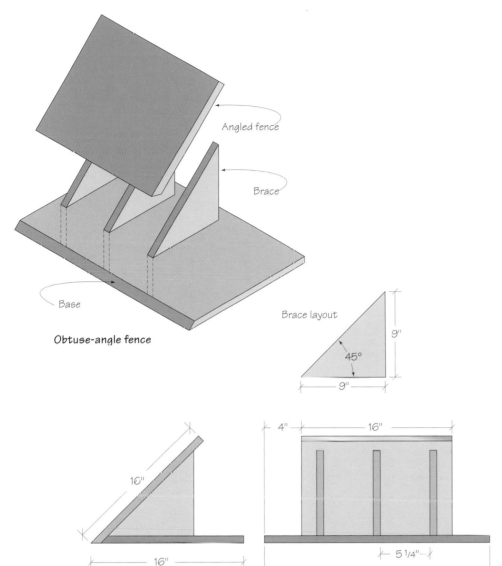

Angled fence

Brace

Base

Obtuse-angle fence

Brace layout

9"

45°

9"

16"

16"

4"   16"

5 1/4"

24"

To use the obtuse-angle fence, position it so the slot is where you want it to be on the edge of the workpiece, and clamp it to the tabletop. When the fence is set, prop a work sample on the fence and use it to position the trap fence. Make sure the two fences are parallel.

Cutting a groove is as simple as pushing the work through the channel between the fences. A narrow workpiece that you're slotting across its end may "walk" rather than slide smoothly. Back it up with a large piece of scrap to keep it square (and to back up the cut).

THE OBTUSE-ANGLE FENCE

From time to time, you'll have to deal with a workpiece that's large and too unwieldy for the acute-angle fence. An obtuse-angle fence, which is very similar to the table-saw angle sled, provides much better support and eases the job of grooving these larger pieces. Use it in conjunction with a separate trap fence, as shown in the photos.

This fence also can be used to make the grooves with a slot cutter. With your router table's regular fence in place and the slot cutter height properly set, bring the angle fence into position. Make sure it's parallel to the regular fence, with the bottom edge of one fence just kissing the other. Clamp the angle fence to the tabletop.

You make the cut by resting the workpiece on the angle fence with its bevel against the face of the regular fence.

Alter the dimensions to fit your router table and the work. The fence angle can be altered to the suit the job you have to do. Bear in mind that the fence base must extend the back edge of the router table so you can clamp it. The trap fence is a separate piece, positioned and clamped at the front of the router table. By keeping it separate, you can accommodate any thickness of wood.

Cut the fence, base and trap fence to size, and bevel a long edge of each. Miter the braces at the same angle. Assemble the pieces with drywall screws.

Edge-Miter Slotting Fixture

This little fixture is great for slotting edge miters, even when the workpiece is large.

Because the trap fence is integral to the gizmo, setup is fast and frustration-free. Install the bit in the router. Adjust the bit extension above the tabletop to about $1\frac{1}{8}$", so it will project $\frac{3}{8}$" above the base of the fixture.

Make a test cut and adjust the bit or fixture to place the slot exactly where you want it. Cutting the work is as simple as switching on the router, catching the beveled edge in the fixture's channel, then pushing it steadily across the bit.

The edge-miter slotting fixture captures the beveled edge of the workpiece and channels it across a straight bit. Clamped to the tabletop, the fixture controls even large panels so you can use both hands to set the work in place and feed it through the cut.

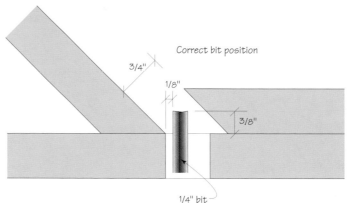

Correct bit position

3/4"

1/8"

3/8"

1/4" bit

Set the fixture over the bit, with the nose of the angled fence $\frac{1}{8}$" from the bit. Sight through the channel as you make this adjustment. Clamp the fixture at the front and the back.

Edge-miter slotting fixture

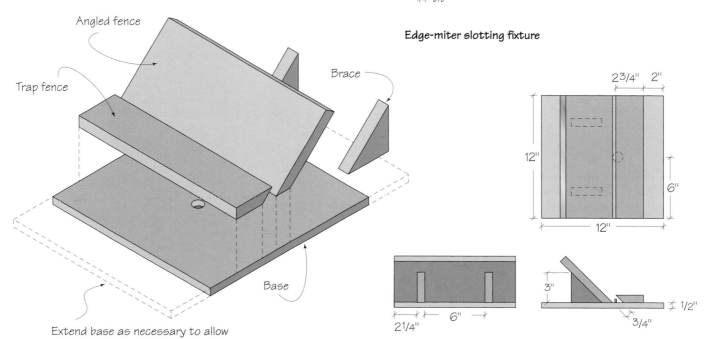

Angled fence

Trap fence

Brace

Base

Extend base as necessary to allow clamping to tabletop at front and back.

23/4"   2"

12"

6"

12"

21/4"

6"

3"

1/2"

3/4"

The model shown was made from scraps of $\frac{3}{4}$" MDF. (The thickness of the base limits the depth of cut somewhat, but you're not going much deeper than $\frac{1}{2}$" in edge-mitered $\frac{3}{4}$" stock.) Construction is simple. Because MDF splits easily when screws are driven into its edges, I used plywood for the braces.

Make the base large enough for you to clamp it to your router tabletop. Bore the bit opening first, then align the angled fence tangent to it. The trap fence can hold the tip of this fence while you drive screws through it into the base. Install the braces. Then use a scrap of plywood as a gauge to position and mount the trap fence.

With the work sandwiched face-to-face, you can guide a trim router along one bevel while the slot cutter in its collet grooves the other bevel. Use an oversized bearing, positioned beneath the cutter plate, to limit the depth of the cut.

The grain in a solid-wood spline must run parallel to the grain in the parts being assembled. If you don't have a single piece as wide as the groove is long, simply tuck the pieces you do have edge to edge as you work along the groove.

Handheld Router Grooving

Splined joinery isn't the exclusive province of stationary tools. With a router and slot cutter, you can do the grooves for most every splined joint. A few of the joints can be done with a straight bit, but to do it you generally must fit the tool with an edge guide, then balance it on the workpiece edge and, well, it gets complicated.

With a slot cutter, on the other hand, the router sits on the face of the workpiece while the cutter works the edge. The slotter has a pilot bearing and you can switch bearings to get the depth of cut you want.

If you have a small router (such as a trimmer), you can use it with a slot cutter to groove ends and flat miters. Even edge and end miters can be grooved with this setup. Clamp two workpieces face to face, so the bevels

angle to the outside. Rest the router on one bevel, and the slotter cuts a groove in the adjacent one.

The biggest challenge with all these approaches is the handling and clamping that's necessary.

Assembly

First the splines have to be fitted. Plywood splines are easy; simply cut them to width and length. If the spline is stopped or blind, the ends of the splines usually must be rounded to fit.

A wood spline is planed to thickness, then ripped and crosscut to fit. If the slots are stopped or blind, ends must be shaped. For an end or flat miter, the spline's grain runs at right angles to the joint's seam. Crosscut strips of a long blank and glue them side by side in the slot in one part,

then assemble the joint.

Assembly usually is uncomplicated: spread glue, insert spline, close joint, apply clamps.

The real payoff comes in assembling a miter joint. Typically, miters are difficult to get into alignment and, as clamps are applied and tightened, to keep in alignment. That is seldom the case when the miter is splined. The spline prevents the faces of the bevels from slipping and sliding. You still have to apply clamps with glued-on, tacked-on or clamped-on cleats so the pressure is directed across the joint, but the splines make the operations a whole lot easier.

Ease of assembly is the whole point of the spline, and it works.

SLIDING DOVETAIL JOINTS

For the woodworker building furniture and cabinets, the sliding dovetail is a joint well worth mastering. It's strong and versatile, with myriad applications from case construction to leg-and-rail joinery. It has a long history of use.

This attractive joint is a hybrid of the dado and the dovetail, with a groove in one part, a tongue on the other. Naturally, the tongue fits the groove. But because both the groove walls and the tongue sides are angled like a dovetail, the joint has to be assembled by sliding the tongue into the groove from one end.

The sliding dovetail joint offers several advantages. Assembling a chest with several drawer dividers is simple when the parts lock together. You don't need five hands and a bunch of clamps.

Instead, simply drive a divider into the slot in one side and the two parts will stay connected. Tip up the second side, hold it with one hand while you lift the divider with the other and catch the tail in the slot. Now your hands are free to wield a mallet, set the other dividers in place or scratch your nose.

Once the chest is assembled, the joint mechanically resists tension, meaning the sides can't bulge outward and off the dividers.

The joint offers advantages in other applications as well. If left unglued, it allows the parts to move without coming apart. A good example of this can be seen at the end of a breadboard. Attached across the end of a broad, solid-wood panel like a chest lid or a tabletop, the breadboard's end is intended to keep the panel flat, attached in such a way that the panel can expand and contract with humidity changes.

Here's how it works: You groove the breadboard end and cut a tongue across the end of the panel. Slide the end onto the tongue without glue. The end strip prevents the panel from bowing, but it won't restrict movement.

You can fix the breadboard end at one edge of the panel with a little glue applied as the joint closes, or at the center by driving a dowel or brad through the joint. If the end strip is fixed at an edge, the panel's movement will show at the opposite edge. If fixed in the center, the movement will show equally at both edges.

Other applications of the sliding dovetail abound:

• Join shelves to bookcase sides.

• Build drawers, joining the sides to the front — and even the back — to the sides.

• Join aprons to table legs and even

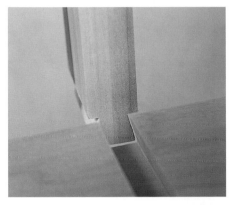

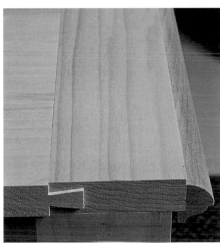

The sliding dovetail is excellent for mounting a breadboard end on a chest lid. Glue it at the front only, and seasonal expansion and contraction of the lid panel will be visible only at the back. Flush with the end of the breadboard when assembled in midwinter, this lid panel expanded markedly over a humid summer.

rails to stiles in frame-and-panel constructions.

• Mount moldings and case tops with dovetail keys or butterfly keys, holding them tight to the structure but allowing the wood to move.

• Mount battens to lids and doors to prevent them from bowing (the same technique used to mount a breadboard end).

• Make drawer runners and guides.

• Construct extension-table slides.

Laborious to cut by hand, it's a relative snap to produce with a router (or two).

Each sliding dovetail joint requires two operations: cutting the groove and cutting the tail. Both operations are

Here's the benefit of the sliding dovetail: The inward slanting walls of the dovetail groove prevent the tail from popping straight out. To assemble the joint, slide the tail into the groove from the end.

Battens fitted to a wide panel with sliding dovetails keep it flat without restricting its seasonal movement. Designed to resemble two drawer fronts, this computer desk door is very wide in terms of grain direction and surely would cup without the battens. No glue or fasteners used here.

done with the router, and to get a good fit, it's imperative to use the same bit for both.

Make the grooves with a handheld or table-mounted router. The location of the cut and the size of the cut itself usually dictates which approach is optimum.

You can cut the tails either way. The portable router generally requires jigging to steady it on the narrow edge being worked. As a consequence, most woodworkers cut the tails on the router table. There you need nothing beyond all-purpose accessories like a push block and a featherboard or two.

CHOOSING A BIT

Dovetail bits are made in a variety of diameters and angles. Most half-blind dovetail jigs require a $\frac{1}{2}$" diameter 14° bit on a $\frac{1}{4}$" shank, so I'd say that's the most common bit. But thanks to the prevalence of through-dovetail jigs, you can buy bits with 7° tapers, as well as with $7\frac{1}{2}$°, 8° and 9° tapers. These angles yield more of a hand-cut look.

A benefit of these bits — one that's pertinent here — is that they allow deeper cuts. Check out the comparison drawing. A $\frac{1}{2}$" diameter, 14° bit can cut only $\frac{1}{2}$" deep because, at that point, the bit has tapered to a $\frac{1}{4}$" diameter. At the same spot on an 8° bit, the girth is about $\frac{11}{32}$". When the cut has narrowed to $\frac{1}{4}$", it is $\frac{13}{16}$" deep.

While you can buy bits that are larger and smaller than $\frac{1}{2}$" diameter, that size is optimum for stock between $\frac{3}{4}$" and $\frac{7}{8}$" thick.

SCALING THE JOINT

For casework, a shallow sliding dovetail — say $\frac{1}{8}$" deep, for example — is all you need. Even in a dado joint, that depth is sufficient to withstand the shear stresses applied to a cabinet and its parts. Add the dovetail angle and you reap the mechanical blessings it confers. Yet that cut depth is easy for any router in a single pass.

On the other hand, you'll want the groove in a breadboard end to be as deep as you can make it without compromising the groove-wall thickness or the thickness at the base of the tail.

The joint experiences the greatest stress in a tabletop. If it's likely that someone will lean their elbows heavily on the breadboard end itself, leveraging the joint, I recommend choosing a different joint (multiple mortises and tenons, for example).

Length must be considered when scaling a sliding dovetail. The longer a joint is, the more problematic it is to fit. I don't know if it's anomalies in the wood or just bad karma, but achieving

Dovetail bits are made in a wide variety of diameters, roughly from $\frac{1}{4}$" up to 1". Angles range from 7° to 14°.

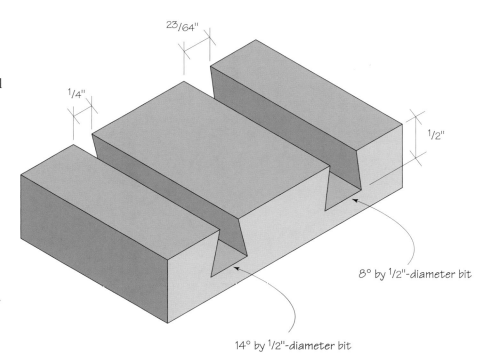

23/64"

1/4"

1/2"

8° by $\frac{1}{2}$"-diameter bit

14° by $\frac{1}{2}$"-diameter bit

Dovetail angle comparison

The steeper the dovetail angle, the less material at the waist of the tail. For a dovetail in casework, where the cut is shallow, this has little impact. But in apron-to-leg or breadboard-end applications, a shallow dovetail angle means the tail can penetrate deeper without becoming too frail at the waist.

a consistent fit along all 24 inches, more or less, of a breadboard-end joint is virtually impossible.

In casework, you would do well to avoid a sliding dovetail that's the full width of a side. It's one thing to make an 8" or 9" sliding dovetail that joins a shelf to a side in a pine bookcase and quite another to assemble a 16" to 18" sliding dovetail in hard maple. Confronted with a joint this length, I suggest a shouldered sliding dovetail, which integrates a shallow through dado with a deeper stopped dovetail at the case front.

Slotting a Face

You can cut slots with portable or table-mounted routers. For casework or bookshelves, I use a portable router, guiding it along a clamped-on straight-edge (a shop-made T-square is perfect).

If you are cutting a $1/8$"-deep slot and using an 8° bit, cut away. If your cut is deeper, for instance $3/8$", and your bit is a 14° taper with a very narrow waist, it's a good idea to "stage" the cut.

A dovetail groove has to be cut in one pass at full depth. There's no way to do it in multiple passes at increasing depths. The way to "stage" such a cut, to reduce the stress on the router and especially the bit, is to rout a groove with a straight bit that matches the dovetail's waist diameter, cutting about $1/16$" shy of the final depth.

In the example situation, you'd use a $1/4$" straight, cutting (perhaps in two passes) about $5/16$" deep. This is most convenient to do if you have two routers of the same base diameter, so you can set one up with the straight bit, the other with the dovetail bit. The fence position for both cuts ends up being the same.

STOPPED SLOTS

The stopped slot presents a feed direction problem. Because of the dovetail

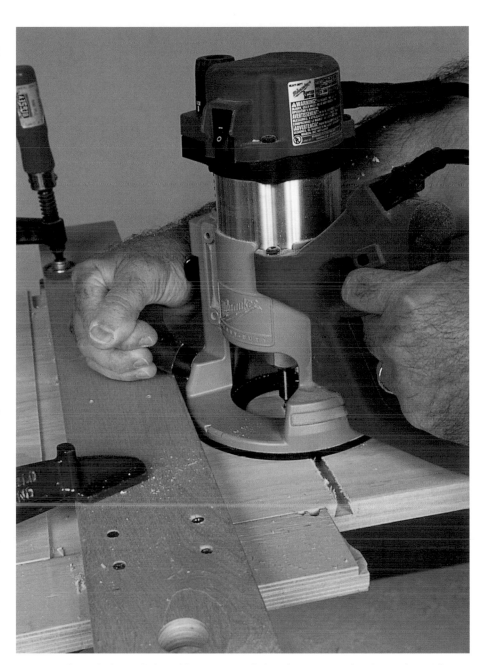

Cutting a through dovetail slot is like routing a dado. Clamp a straightedge to the workpiece, and guide the router along it, cutting from one edge of the work through to the opposite edge.

profile, the cutter is trapped in the cut. Unlike a dado, you can't necessarily begin or end a dovetail groove anywhere.

Consider this common situation. You are making a chest of drawers, and your plan calls for stopped sliding dovetails to join the drawer dividers to the chest sides. Typically, you lay out the two sides simultaneously, so cuts on the right side perfectly align with cuts on the left side. The process prob-

ably goes as far as marking locations for the fence along which you'll guide the router.

Here's the feed direction problem. On one side the correct feed is from the edge into the slot's terminus. But on the other, the correct feed is from the terminus out to the edge. Again, because of the dovetail profile, you'll probably want to make all the cuts by feeding in from the edge, then carefully backing the cutter out of the slot.

On every stopped cut you make, you'll be feeding the router in the wrong direction part of the time. Remember that when you feed in the correct direction, the spinning bit's rotational forces help keep the tool against the guide. When you feed in the wrong direction — when you make a climb cut, in other words — those rotational forces want to pull the tool away from the guide. When you rout a stopped dovetail slot, there's a risk of the bit grabbing somewhere along the cut and pulling the router off the fence. That would ruin the cut.

I know woodworkers who rout along a fence, maintaining enough force to keep the router against the fence. You can try that approach, of course, and may have success with it.

A simple alternative is to plow the cut to the stopping point, then switch off the router. Let it wind down, then back the bit out of the cut. But this works only for one side of that chest-of-drawers project. The initial cuts on the second side are the climb cuts. You can't make those with the router switched off.

An outrageous alternative is to simply pop the bit out of the cut or plunge it into the cut. The cut will look odd, like the bulb at the bottom of an old mercury thermometer. But a $\frac{1}{2}$"-diameter bit makes a $\frac{1}{2}$"-diameter hole, and in the assembled joint, the hole will be concealed by a $\frac{3}{4}$"-thick tail board. Without the taper at the end of the slot, you will sacrifice some of the joint's strength, but I don't think it's enough to undermine the joint's overall integrity, so long as the tail-to-slot fit is precise.

All that said, I prefer to make stopped cuts with the router trapped, either between a pair of fences or with a template. If the router is trapped, it can't wander, regardless of the feed direction. With either guide system, I can plow into the cut, then back out, with the router running all the while.

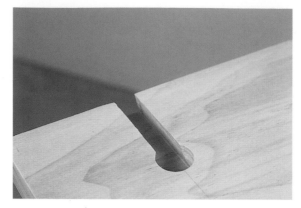

Plunging a dovetail bit into a cut (or popping it out of the cut) isn't the conventional way to begin or end a stopped dovetail cut. Because of the bit profile, this causes a bulb in the cut's surface contour. But surprise! The shoulders of the tail board cover the bulb completely.

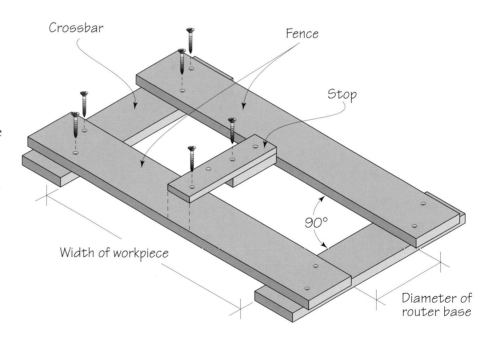

Twin fence guide

A twin-fence guide is a versatile device used for dadoing as well as for sliding dovetail cuts. The two fences trap the router and prevent it from wandering, regardless of the feed direction.

Scale the guide to the job and to your router(s). Scrounge up the parts from your scraps and "shorts" collection. Use hardwood, plywood, MDF or whatever you have. Assemble with drywall screws. Be sure the fences are parallel, the crossbars are parallel and fences are square to the crossbars. The stop is optional.

The twin fence is excellent for this work. If you use it with a $1/2$" bit for dadoing, there's no problem using a $1/2$" dovetail bit with it. If you have such a jig, use it. Failing that, bear in mind that cobbling together a twin-fence guide or a template takes 15 minutes, 20 at most. For the former, you need four strips of plywood or MDF and a few drywall screws. Attach a stop to one or both fences to limit the length of the cut.

A template made from a piece of $1/4$" hardboard will do. Simply rout a slot in from one edge. Make the slot the width of the template guide you'll use. Extend it no longer than necessary to get the length of slot you want.

The template approach has several advantages. You can use any two routers, since the template guide is the registration device, not the router base.

A twin-fence guide eliminates most of the risk in the cutting of dovetail slots, especially stopped ones. If you have two routers with the same base diameter, you can use one for the "wasting" cut (with a straight bit), the other with the dovetail bit.

The jig traps the router, preventing it from drifting off the cutting line even when the feed direction makes it a climb cut. With a stop attached, the router can cut only as far as you want it to.

After roughing the slot with a straight bit, switch to the router with the dovetail bit and make the final cut. The guide ensures all slots will be uniform.

A template provides positive control of the router for uniform stopped cuts. The (walnut) strip clamped to the front edge of the work is waste, intended to prevent tear-out or chipping. The overhang along the front edge ensures that the template guide is caught in the guide slot while the bit is still clear of the work. (The fuzzies on the work's surface are common and easily removed with sandpaper.)

This template aids you in locating multiple slots in pairs of case sides. Here's how to make one. It's is easy to make and doesn't cost much.

Cut the template blank to match the size of the case side. Hardboard is cheap, so this isn't a big investment. Cut the guide slot in the hardboard on the center line of the uppermost slot. Rout the slots in both sides (or in both pairs of sides, whatever is the situation). To align it for a cut, flush the template edges with the workpiece edges. You can use either face of the template to guide a cut, so the same template works for rights and lefts.

To rout the next set of slots, cut down the template. If the distance from one slot center to the next is 7", just saw 7" off the bottom end of the template. Align it the same way and rout all the slots in all workpieces. Then cut it down again.

The slots in the lefts will align with those in the rights. You don't have to lay out each slot. When you set up any of these jigs, be sure to clamp a strip of scrap tight to the edge of the work. Doing so prevents the edge from splintering, something that's almost guaranteed to occur.

To aid you in sizing the tails that will fit into the slots, use your setup to cut a slot in a scrap of the working stock. When you do so, you avoid having to fit the test-cut tails to a slot in a case side itself.

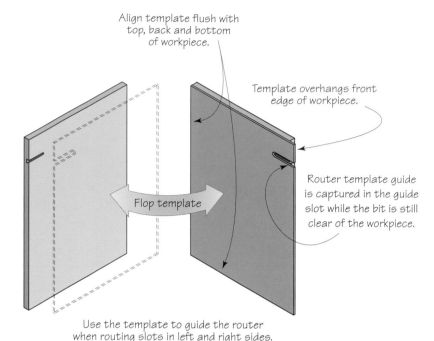

Align template flush with top, back and bottom of workpiece.

Template overhangs front edge of workpiece.

Router template guide is captured in the guide slot while the bit is still clear of the workpiece.

Flop template

Use the template to guide the router when routing slots in left and right sides.

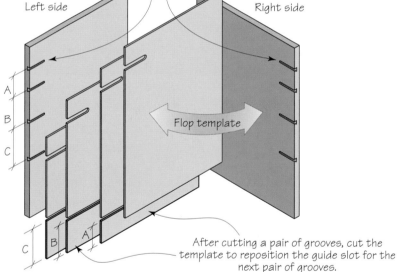

Left side

Right side

Flop template

After cutting a pair of grooves, cut the template to reposition the guide slot for the next pair of grooves.

A hardboard template for routing stopped dovetail slots is inexpensive and easy to make. You can use a single template to slot both the lefts and the rights.

Match it to the dimensions of your case side with about 1" of overhang on the front edge. The overhang allows you to clamp a waste strip to the front edge of the work to prevent tear-out or chipping. It also ensures that the template guide is caught in the guide slot while the bit is still clear of the work.

Locate the guide slot where the side's uppermost slot is to be. Rout this guide slot using a bit that's the size of the template guide you intend to use. After routing that uppermost slot in both the left and the right sides, cut the template down to locate the next pair of dovetail slots.

Cutting a Tail

This is always done across an end or along an edge and is most commonly done on the router table. There are some alternatives, of course, but I'll focus on the router table approach.

Use the same bit you used to make the tails to make the slots. This guarantees the geometry will match.

Close down the bit openings in the tabletop and fence as much as possible. For the tabletop opening, use the appropriate reducer in your router mounting plate or a ⅛" hardboard auxiliary tabletop. For the fence, either close split facings in against the bit or apply a one-piece auxiliary facing and cut a zero-clearance opening with the bit.

Set the height of the bit above the table to match the depth of the groove or slot. If you cut the slots on the router table, move directly from that to the tail cut without changing the bit setting. If you cut the slots with a portable router, use your cut sample as an aid in setting the bit height. You'll "prove" the setting with test cuts, of course.

Bring the fence into position, housing all but the very edge of the bit in the fence. If the workpiece is larger, you may want to add a tall facing to the fence. However, I've found a well-placed featherboard (and my regular fence) is all I need for even big pieces.

A tail is cut in two passes. Cut across one face, turn the workpiece around and cut across the second face. Now you have a tail.

How do you control the size?

First, establish the distance from end to shoulder — the height of the tail. That must match the depth of the slot you've already cut. This is a function of the bit extension. When you adjust this, you must account for the platform thickness — ¼" that separates the work from the router base. I use a rule for the initial setup, then adjust as necessary based on a test cut.

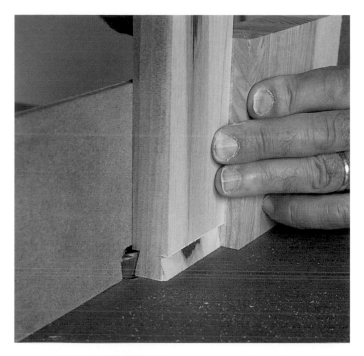

Cut a tail on a narrow piece like a drawer divider by standing it on end, backing it up with a scrap block and advancing it along the fence. The back-up block minimizes exit splintering and helps stabilize the work, reducing its tendency to "walk" along the fence. Make a cut, spin the work 180° and cut again to form the tail.

For a stopped slot, trim one edge of the tail. Simply turn the piece to register its edge against the fence. Use the back-up block, and cut.

The tail — this one intended for a stopped slot — has crisp, uniform-width shoulders on three sides. To nest the end of the tail against the end of the slot, pare the sharp corners with a chisel.

One well-placed feather-board stabilizes even a large panel standing on end. The featherboard is aligned just ahead of the bit and is elevated with a block underneath so it presses above the cut. The fence is the one I use regularly; something taller isn't necessary.

RIGHT-ANGLE PLATFORM

Cutting across the ends of long, narrow pieces is troublesome compared to cutting a big panel. Some folks are wary of trying it on the router table, but what are the alternatives?

Of those that come to mind, the best is a shop-made right-angle platform. To use it, you rest the router on the platform and guide it along an adjustable fence. The bit cuts across the face or edge of the workpiece, which is secured beneath the platform with its end up against the platform's underside.

The platform, I should point out, can be used in cutting elements for other joints, such as tenons and half-laps. It's not a one-use jig.

The dimensions and the construction are shown in the drawing, along with some tips on building it.

To use the platform, you clamp it in a vise so you have ready access to the toggle clamps. The workpiece is tucked against the fence and up against the underside of the platform, then secured with the toggles. Adjust the bit extension and the guide fence position, and rout.

When it comes to fine-tuning the bit extension, you are at the mercy of your router. Most current models offer pretty good microadjustment.

The tail width is established by the location of the fence. The fence is also set initially with a rule. Start by determining the distance from the edge of the router base to the cutting edge of the bit. (This is simple math: Subtract the bit diameter from the base diameter and divide the difference in half.) That's the distance from the fence to the cut, so measure that distance from the cut line on the workpiece to position the fence.

Make sure the fence is parallel to the cut line, which is to say, the front edge of the platform. That would be square to the sides of the platform, so use a try square referencing the side to align the fence as you set the distance

Right angle platform

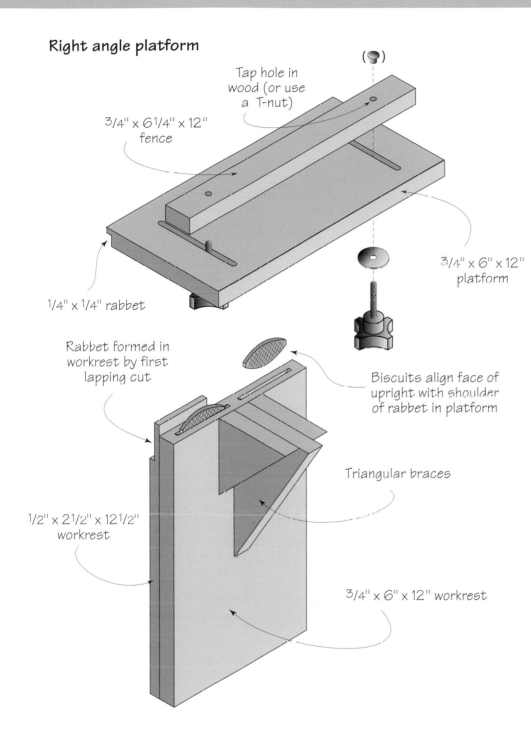

Tap hole in wood (or use a T-nut)

(🔩)

3/4" x 6 1/4" x 12" fence

1/4" x 1/4" rabbet

3/4" x 6" x 12" platform

Rabbet formed in workrest by first lapping cut

Biscuits align face of upright with shoulder of rabbet in platform

Triangular braces

1/2" x 2 1/2" x 12 1/2" workrest

3/4" x 6" x 12" workrest

The right-angle platform is useful in cutting tenons and laps and tails for sliding dovetail joints. It's best used with a fixed-base router, but it isn't customized for any particular size of router.

It's critical, as you assemble the fixture, to have the platform square, the upright perpendicular to the platform and the edge of the platform parallel to the face of the upright. If these aspects of the fixture are imprecise, your cuts also will be imprecise.

The choice of materials isn't critical, though you do want the parts to be flat and true. I used scraps of Baltic birch plywood for the body and hardwood offcuts for the fence and reference block. You can use carriage bolts and wing nuts to mount the fence, though I tapped holes in the fence and threaded shop brewed studded plastic knobs into them. (Cut threaded rod to length and "glue" it into a plastic knob with Loctite®.)

from the front.

Incremental adjustments in fence position are easy to make using the reference block and shims of various thicknesses.

To increase the cut into the workpiece, you must move the fence away from the platform edge. Slide the block up to the fence, drop a shim between the two, then secure the block. Loosen the fence, remove the shim and push the fence tight against the block. Retighten the fence. You've moved the fence an amount equal to the shim thickness.

To decrease the cut, move the fence toward the platform edge. Secure the block tight against the fence. Loosen the fence, insert the shim, push the fence tight and resecure it. Again, you've moved the fence an amount equal to the shim thickness.

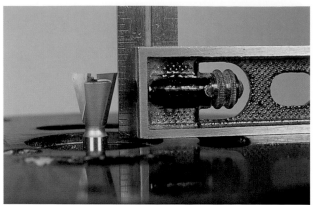

Set the initial depth of cut with the router standing on its head and a square or depth gauge sitting on the router base beside the bit. Account for the platform thickness as well as the actual dimension in your setting.

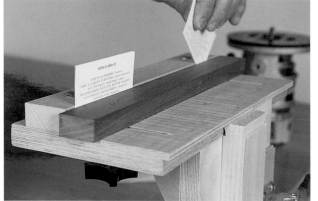

The cut is a conventional edge-forming operation. Make a shallow climb cut first to score the shoulder and eliminate chipping and tearout. Then work the router back and forth until it is tight against the fence throughout a pass. Unclamp, turn and reclamp the work. Cut the second face in the same way, completing the tail.

Want to adjust the tail width by a few thousandths? Use shims between the guide fence and the reference block. This low-tech method enables you to adjust the fence in or out in micro-fine increments.

The right-angle platform makes end cuts possible with a portable router. The jig is held in a bench vise. Its toggle clamps and vertical fence hold a narrow workpiece perpendicular to the router. The platform provides solid bearing for the router, so it's less likely to wobble or tip as you move it through a cut.

Measure from the outer face of the workpiece to set the fence. I use a small square with the blade set at the desired measurement. With the body against the work, I move the fence against the tip of the blade. Measure from both edges of the work to ensure the fence is parallel to the work.

FITTING THE TAIL TO THE SLOT

Regardless of your tail-cutting approach, the drill is the same. Make a test cut on a scrap of the working stock. The scrap must be exactly the same thickness as the real work. I think it's most effective to creep up on the fit. That is, start with a "fat" tail and check it against the grooved sample. Make a fence position adjustment,

recut (both sides of the tail) and recheck the fit. I keep trimming the initial sample until I get the right fit. My final assessment, however, is based on a fresh sample.

How tight you make the fit depends on the application. A short joint, such as one that joins a drawer divider to a case side, should close at least halfway with hand pressure and require only a

tap or two to seat. You'll be able to assemble it with glue, and the glue line will look nice and tight.

If you have to pound the tail into the slot, it's too tight for gluing. If it slides home with firm hand pressure, the fit isn't ideal, but the joint will hold well when glued. Finally, if the tail piece slides into the slot easily, and especially if it wiggles from side to side, you need to start over. The tail is too small.

The most problematic joint to fit is a long one, such as a breadboard end. You aren't going to glue it (except at one end), because it is cross-grained. You do want it tight, so the seam at the shoulder isn't gappy. But as the tail slides through the groove, the friction builds, and even without glue it can be tough to drive home. Obviously, you want to assemble this joint only once.

So how do you test the fit without assembling the joint? Use your final test cut samples as gauges.

Slide the groove sample onto the tail and work it from one end to the other. This should help you isolate really tight sections, where you may want to sand or pare the tail. Do this on each long tail.

Likewise, slide the tail sample through each long groove.

A long tail that's to mate with a long slot is the most problematic to fit. You want to assemble the joint only once, but you don't want it to seize an inch or two shy of the end. Best testing option is to use short gauges, one with the final dimension groove, another with the final tail, to pass across — or through — the full tail or groove.

DOVETAIL JOINTS

Dovetails are prime joints: long history, great appearance, cachet. Used in boxes, drawers, carcasses. But for many woodworkers, cutting dovetails the traditional way — with saw and chisels — is an insurmountable challenge.

The half-blind dovetail jig makes and cuts pins and tails at the same time with the same bit. This model has a rigid extruded aluminum base and a durable phenolic template. During extended dovetailing sessions, its large knobs are easier on the hands than the wing nuts found on cheap jigs. The jig is mounted on a shop-made platform that expands workpiece support and incorporates positioning fences on the front and the top.

Routing Dovetails

The router can help. Sure, hand-cutting advocates like to argue that in the time it takes to master any of the router dovetail jigs you can master handcutting. (Not true, I say!) But as a counterpoint, I think of my friend Ken. He's proficient at the hand-tool approach, yet he recently bought a sophisticated dovetail jig primarily to boost his productivity.

If you aren't ready to tackle handcut dovetails, if power-assisted woodworking is for you, there are plenty of router accessories on the market to help you. There are so many in fact, and so many variations in setup and operation, that I'm going to narrow my focus to the most common: the half-blind dovetail jig.

The typical half-blind dovetail jig consists of a metal base with two clamping bars to hold the workpieces.

A comb-like template rests on the top to guide the router in cutting both pieces at once.

The biggest differences from brand to brand and model to model are the quality of the materials and hardware, as well as the precision with which the jig is made and assembled. The cheap ones have stamped parts that tend to flex and buckle, threads that strip quite easily and wing nuts that chew at your fingers. The model shown in the photos has a rigid extruded aluminum base and a durable phenolic template. Its large clamp knobs are easy on the hands during extended dovetailing sessions. Some jigs have an extra template for ¼" half-blind dovetails, and a few have them for ¼" and ½" box joints as well.

In addition to the jig, you need a router, a ½"-diameter by 14°-bevel dovetail bit and a guide bushing, usu-

ally ⁷⁄₁₆"-diameter in size, though occasionally a larger bushing is called for. The appropriate bit and guide are typically packaged with the jig, and in most instances, you'll find they are generic. Because the working end of the bit is larger than the opening in the template guide, you have to install it after the template guide. That means there's benefit in using a long-shanked bit, but that's not usually what is packaged with the jig.

You can use any router. I've routed dovetails with a laminate trimmer, but typically I use a 1½- to 2-horsepower fixed-base model. The ability to plunge is irrelevant in this operation, and plunge routers generally are awkward for work done on the edge (which this work is) owing to their high centers of gravity. Brute power doesn't contribute much, if anything. But don't buy a new router just for dovetailing.

Dovetail jigs cut left hand and right hand dovetails. This means you need to mark the parts so you insert them into the jig properly. The top edges of your parts must always be oriented to the outside with the inner surfaces exposed. Thus, the joints on the left of your assembly must be cut on the left end of the jig (left), while the right side joints must be cut on the jig's right (right). Methodically marking the parts, as well as drawing a setup diagram on the jig, helps reduce goof-ups that waste materials and time.

Organizing the parts

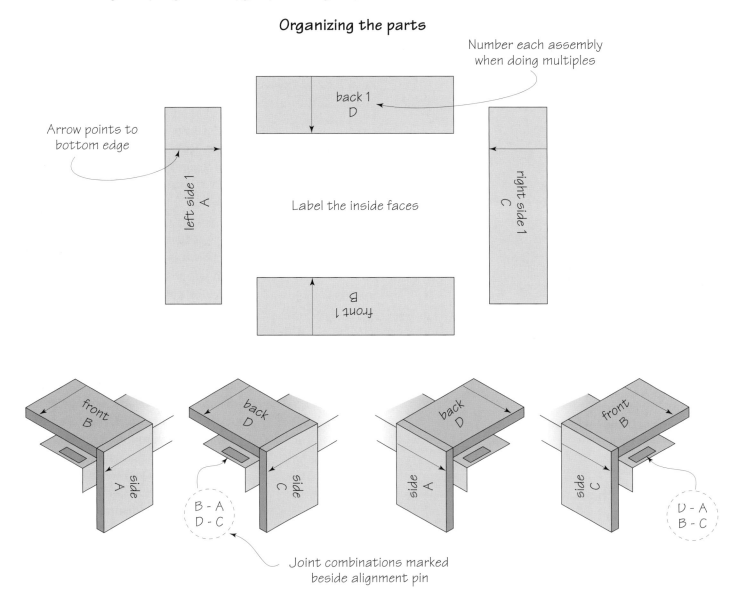

Number each assembly when doing multiples

back 1
D

Arrow points to bottom edge

left side 1
A

Label the inside faces

right side 1
C

front 1
B

front
B

side
A

back
D

side
C

B - A
D - C

back
D

side
A

front
B

side
C

D - A
B - C

Joint combinations marked beside alignment pin

HALF-LAP

JOINTS

A half-lap is strong, versatile and easy to cut. To make one, you cut recesses in both mating pieces, then nest them together, forming an *X*, *L* or *T*.

Half-laps are used to make all sorts of flat frames. Doors, for example, but also face frames, web frames and picture frames. An intermediate rail half-lapped to the stiles looks right, because it visually abuts the stile (the way a mortise and tenon would) rather than crossing it (the way a bridle joint would). On the other hand, a rectangle of end grain is exposed in assembled end laps and T-laps, which you may regard as unsightly.

Lap joinery

The half lap (or its kin, the full lap) is used in post and rail constructions to join rails or aprons to legs. You usually see this joinery in worktables rather than fine furniture. But even in the most traditional table construction, the half lap is used where stretchers cross (a cross lap).

From a practical perspective, the half-lap joint enjoys a big advantage over the mortise and tenon in that one tool setup suffices for both parts of some forms of the joint. (There's more than one form of half lap, of course, and T-laps in particular require two setups, as you'll see.) You can join parts at angles quite easily. The joint accommodates curved parts too. You can join curved pieces, or you can shape the half-lapped frame after it's assembled.

Despite its simplicity, this joint is very strong if properly made. The shoulders of the half lap provide resistance to twisting. In addition, the laps provide plenty of long-grain to long-grain gluing surface.

Be wary of using half-laps on wide boards. Wood movement can break the joint, so confine the joinery to members no more than 3" to 3½" wide.

You can rough out laps with a circular saw, a radial-arm saw, a miter saw or a band saw. You can cut smooth, square laps on the table saw or with a router, either handheld or table-mounted. Let the particulars of the job suggest a tool to use and a way to use it too.

There are two basic half-lap cuts: the end lap and the cross lap. The end lap is far easier to cut, and you can cut it with any of the tools I mentioned. The cross lap is more limiting because you can't address the end of the workpiece. The most sensible way to explain the joint-cutting options is according to tool setup.

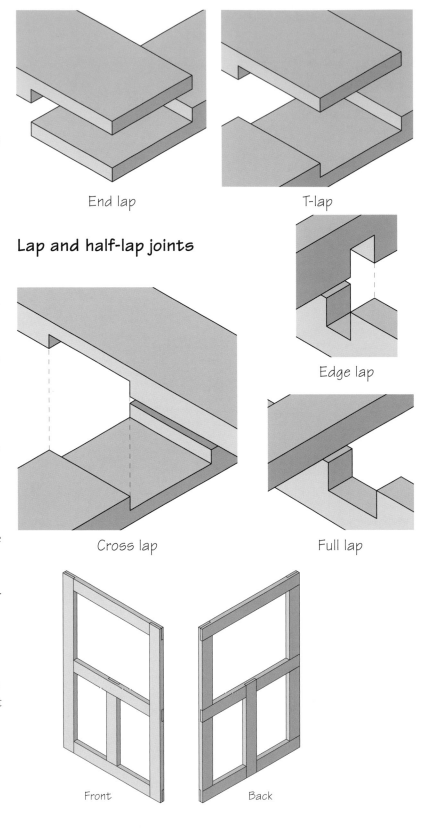

End lap

T-lap

Lap and half-lap joints

Cross lap

Edge lap

Full lap

Half-lapped frame

Front

Back

From one side — call it the front — a frame assembled with half-lap joints looks like a conventional mortise-and-tenon construction. The rail ends meet the edges of the stiles, the muntin ends meet the edges of the rails. The appearance meets your expectations. But from the other side, the look defies expectations.

Stop plate

Router table tenoning sled

Stop jaw

Carriage bolt T-nut Stop jaw Jam nut

Wingnut

Fence

Stop clamp assembly

Shoe

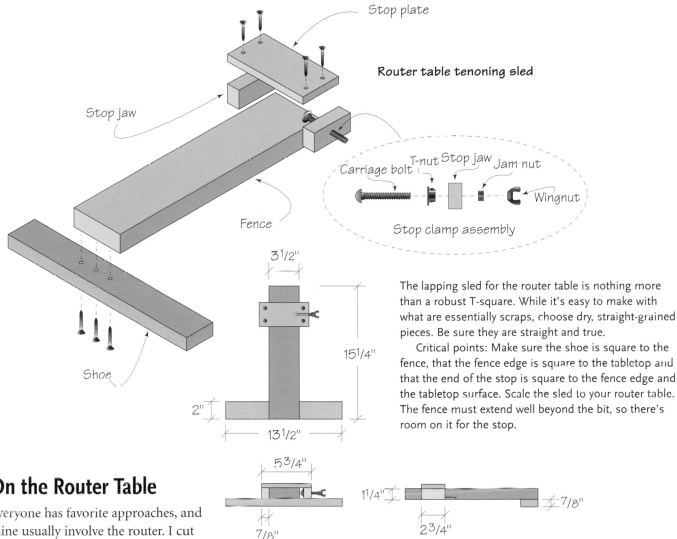

3½"

15¼"

2"

13½"

The lapping sled for the router table is nothing more than a robust T-square. While it's easy to make with what are essentially scraps, choose dry, straight-grained pieces. Be sure they are straight and true.

Critical points: Make sure the shoe is square to the fence, that the fence edge is square to the tabletop and that the end of the stop is square to the fence edge and the tabletop surface. Scale the sled to your router table. The fence must extend well beyond the bit, so there's room on it for the stop.

5¾"

7/8"

1¼"   7/8"

2¾"

On the Router Table

Everyone has favorite approaches, and mine usually involve the router. I cut end laps on the router table using a guide I originally made for tenoning. This shop-made device looks like a T-square on steroids. The stout fence is long enough to extend from the table-top edge to well beyond the bit. The crossbar rides along the edge of the tabletop. A stop clamps to the fence to control the length of the cut.

Construction is simple, but pay attention to the details. The fence must be square to the crossbar. The edge of the fence must be perpendicular to the tabletop. The stop also must be square to the fence. If any of these angles are off, you won't get consistently sized, square-shouldered laps.

You can scale the jig to reference whichever tabletop edge you prefer. The front edge is what I use, but you could reference the end or the back edge.

This rudimentary sled, used with the saddle-type stop and the mortising bit installed in the table-mounted router, produces smooth, crisp-shouldered laps (and tenons). The sled can reference any edge of the table that suits you.

What bit to use? A straight bit is the obvious choice and will work fine here. I use what's variously called a planer, mortising or bottom-cleaning bit. The several I have range in diameter from $\frac{3}{4}$" up to $1\frac{1}{2}$", and the vertical cutting edges range from $\frac{7}{16}$" up to $\frac{7}{8}$". The bit is designed to clear a wide, smooth recess. Perfect for laps!

The first time you use this lapping guide, you'll cut into the fence. This cut is what you use to position the stop for the length of lap you want. Measure from the shoulder of the cut (remember to include the cut itself in the measurement). The stop prevents you from making a cut that's too long.

Be mindful of the size of the cut and the amount of material you will remove in a pass. You don't necessarily want to hog out a $\frac{3}{8}$"-deep cut in a single pass, especially if you are using a $1\frac{1}{4}$"-to $1\frac{1}{2}$"-diameter bit.

There are two ways to moderate the bite: Reduce the depth of the cut or the width of the cut. Here, the most expeditious approach is the latter. Form the full cut in small steps. The first pass should be about $\frac{1}{8}$" wide — hold the workpiece well clear of the stop so only $\frac{1}{8}$" extends over the bit. Make pass after pass, shifting the workpiece closer and closer to the stop. One last pass with the workpiece dead against the stop and your lap is completed.

The easiest way to stage a cut with the lapping sled is to nibble into the cut from the end. Set the bit to the correct setting for the full-depth cut. Hold the workpiece well shy of the stop and cut a narrow rabbet across the end (top). Move the work closer to the stop for the second pass (middle), then butt it against the stop for the final pass (bottom). (The process generates a lot of dirt.)

The cut surface is smooth and flat, perfect for gluing. If the depth and length are correct, no additional paring or fitting is needed

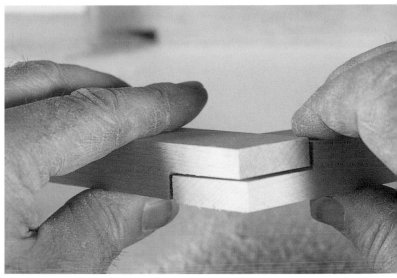

Cut a pair of samples and assemble the joint. I like to have the faces of mating parts come flush as the joint closes, so I only have to finish sanding.

Mortising bits are made in a range of diameters, with and without shank-mounted pilot bearings. All produce a smooth-bottom, square-shouldered cut. Use the bit without a bearing in the router table, with the bearing in a portable router.

This approach works well for end laps, less so for laps midway between the ends of the workpiece. The fence isn't long, so you can't use the stop to position the work for a cross-lap cut. By eye, it's tough to line up the work for an accurately placed cut. (You could make a guide with an extended fence, but I think a long fence makes it unwieldy for end laps. Compromises, compromises. Maybe you want to make two...)

For a cross- or a T-lap, you'd need to use an accessory like the dadoing sled, shown in the Dado Joints chapter, or the sliding fence, shown in the Sliding Dovetail Joint chapter. With either accessory, you'd use a stop to keep the work from moving as the bit cuts it, something that helps you place the cut as well. Set the stop to position the final cut, and use a spacer between the stop and the work to position the first cut.

Personally, I think it's a pain in the neck to do tees and crosses accurately on the router table. Given my druthers, I'd do them with a handheld router and a job-specific (disposable) jig.

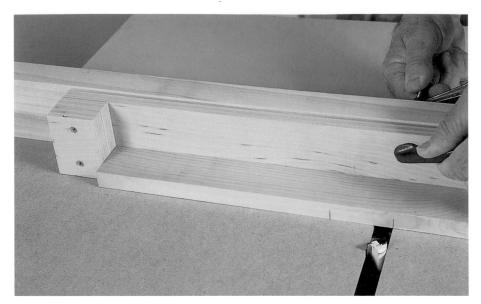

The crosscut sled shown in the Dado Joints chapter can be used for cutting laps. To cut a cross lap like the one marked on the workpiece, align the left shoulder mark with the bit. Slide the stop between the work and the sled fence and bring the stop block against the end of the work. The stop prevents the bit rotation from pulling the workpiece to the right as it cuts. Clamp the stop to the fence.

Spacers inserted between the stop block and the work's end shift the workpiece so the bit aligns with the right shoulder of the intended lap. Two pieces of ¾" MDF used in conjunction with a ¾" bit will produce a 2¼"-wide lap. Make the first cut with both spacers in place. Then remove one for the next pass and the second for the final pass.

Cut a lap and test-fit the mating piece in it. You want it to fit tightly between the shoulders. Too tight? Move the stop to your right and increase the total thickness of the spacers by twice the amount you moved the stop. Too loose? Move the stop to your left and decrease the total thickness of the spacers by twice the amount you moved the stop. (If you do the first without doing the second, you'll simply shift the position of the lap without changing the width of it.)

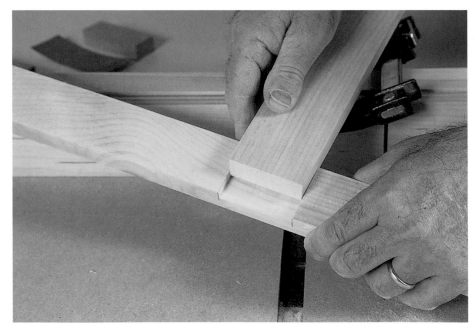

ALTERNATIVE APPROACHES

For end laps on fairly narrow stock, for example 2" or less, you can use a long straight bit, making the cuts as if making a wide rabbet. (Yes, an end-lap is a wide rabbet.) Simply stand the workpiece on end and slide it along the fence to make the cut.

Anything wider than 2" will outstrip the cutting length of the longest straight bits you'll find. You can stretch the reach of any bit by cheating it out of the collet, but that is done with some risk.

Chuck the straight bit in your router and adjust the extension to match the width of the end lap. (Lay a piece of the working stock on edge beside the bit, then raise the bit until its tip aligns flush with the stock's top edge.)

Attach a tall facing, one that will provide good support to a workpiece that's standing on its end to the fence. Move the fence into position, housing the bit almost entirely. You want only $\frac{1}{16}$" to $\frac{1}{8}$" of it exposed, so you will be making a very shallow cut. Lock down the fence.

Support and back up the workpiece with a scrap — one that's flat, true and square. Slide the work along the fence and across the bit, routing a shallow recess. Move the fence back slightly to expose more of the bit, thus increasing the depth of the cut, and make another pass. Repeat this cut-and-adjust routine until you've reached the desired depth.

Cutting a lot of laps this way isn't as efficient as the first approach. The need to adjust and readjust the fence to stage the cuts complicates and slows production.

Were I to use this approach for a great number of identical laps, I'd follow this sequence:
  • Set the final fence position through test-cuts.
  • Capture that position with stops clamped to the tabletop at the fence's back edge.

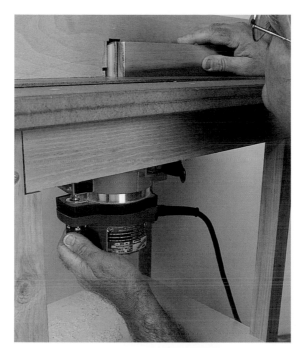

You can cut a half lap on the router table with a straight bit, provided the pieces aren't too wide. The bit must have cutting edges long enough to address the full cut width with each pass. Lay a part to be lapped beside the bit and adjust the bit extension to match the workpiece width, as shown. Note the tight clearance around the bit of the fence facing, which is a strip of $\frac{1}{4}$" plywood mounted with double-sided tape.

Cut the lap with the piece on end and backed up with a scrap pusher. To reduce the load on the router and bit, reduce the bite on the initial pass or two by moving the fence forward (less of the bit is exposed). Closing down the bit opening in the tabletop — here with a hardboard auxiliary top — eliminates the chance that the work will catch on the rim of an oversize hole and stall the cut.

  • Pull the fence forward to reduce the bite and make a first cut on every workpiece.
  • Reposition the fence closer to the stops and make another cut on each workpiece.
  • Set the fence against the stops and make a final pass on each workpiece.

That works better — in my mind — than adjusting the fence two or three times for each individual workpiece.

The lap, straight from the cut, is smooth and will glue exceptionally well.

Handheld Router

I have two different jigs in my kit bag for doing laps with a portable router. One, a right angle platform, is strictly for end laps (but also for other joints, such as tenons and sliding dovetails), while the other, a saddle jig, works for both end and cross laps. The latter is great for angled laps and for lapping curved pieces.

RIGHT-ANGLE PLATFORM

The right-angle platform holds the workpiece upright and provides both a support surface and a guide for the router. A drawing of it and construction information is in the Sliding Dovetail Joints chapter.

Clamp the platform in your bench vise to set it up and use it. The router sits on the platform and rides along the guide fence. The bit extends below the platform and cuts whatever it contacts. (Depending on where you station the guide fence, the bit may trim the edge of the platform itself and the work-rest fence.)

The length of the lap is governed by the extension of the router bit. I've done 2"-long laps comfortably with the setup, using a $\frac{1}{2}$"-diameter bit with 2"-long cutting edges. You have to account for the $\frac{1}{4}$" platform thickness between the router base and the end of the workpiece, but that doesn't rob a lot from the overall capacity.

The depth of the lap is governed by the position of the guide fence. The closer to the platform edge the fence is, the shallower the cut will be. A little math helps you position the fence. Subtract the radius of the bit from the radius of the router base. The difference is the distance from the cut line that the fence must be spotted.

To begin setup, I first mark a line that represents the lap's cheek across the end of the workpiece, then clamp it in the fixture. Next, I choose my bit and do the math. Using a rule or small

The versatile right-angle platform enables you to cut end laps with a portable router and a long straight bit. The stock width cannot exceed the length of the bit's cutting edges. The most critical task is positioning the guide fence. I scribe a cheek line across the end of a work sample, then use a small adjustable square to set the fence, measuring from the line (not the edge of the platform). Measure at each edge of the workpiece, bringing first one end of the fence against the square, then the other.

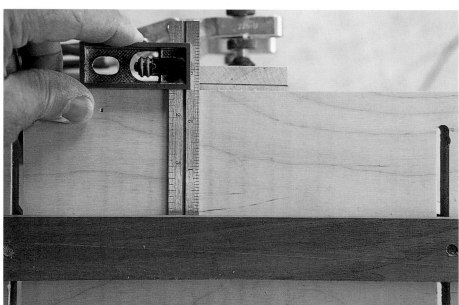

square, I measure from the line on the workpiece and locate the fence. A square referencing the end of the platform aligns the fence. If you err, try to err on the side of a too-shallow cut.

Make a pair of test-cuts, fit the pieces together and check the edges and faces.

Adjust the fence position as necessary. If you need to microadjust use a reference block and shims.

Here's the work routine: First set the workpiece against the fence, its end butted up against the underside of the platform. Secure it with the toggles. Switch on the router and guide it along the fence, cutting the workpiece.

Tear-out along the shoulder of the lap can be pretty damaging if you feed the router in the correct direction. This is one of those instances where a climb cut is both controllable and beneficial.

Cutting the lap is a matter of moving the router back and forth across the platform, nibbling at the waste. You cut the full depth from the outset, of course, so the bit projects dramatically — some might say menacingly — from the router. Make a very shallow climb cut first to score the shoulder of the lap without tear-out. A shallow cut is easily controlled. Make several more passes, widening the cut, until the router rides against the fence throughout a pass.

Here's the first step in assembling a lapping platform: Sandwich a workpiece between the fences, and clamp these parts. Align the primary platform on them. The guide edge of the platform must be square to the work. Screw the platform to the fences.

I generally make a shallow climbing pass, then bring the router back — cutting along the way — and finish up with a final climbing pass. The router is only fully against the fence on the final pass.

LAPPING PLATFORM

The lapping platform is a job-specific jig that fits over a workpiece like a saddle. You make it for a particular job, fitting it to the actual workpieces. All you need are four scraps and a half dozen or so drywall screws.

To cut laps with this jig, I use the same mortising bit that cuts laps with the sled on the router table. The difference is that for this application, I mount a pilot bearing on the shank. I prefer to use a fixed-base router, rather than a plunger.

Begin assembling the jig by clamping the fences to the edges of a workpiece. The fences must be just under the thickness of the workpieces, and their edges must be straight and parallel.

Next, set the main platform on the workpiece and the fences. I usually use

¾" MDF for this, but plywood is OK. Square it, then screw it to the fences.

Finally, lay the second workpiece across the first, tight against the platform's guiding edge. Set the second platform in place and clamp it tight against the second workpiece. Screw it to the fences.

The gap between the platforms is the width of the lap. It's easy to position; just set the platform edges directly on your layout lines. The bearing rides along the edges of the two platforms while the bit just below it excavates the lap. The bit is trapped, so you won't get a lap that's too wide. The fences tight against the workpiece edges prevent tear-out. The platforms support the router and keep it from tipping. Assuming the workpieces are equal in width, you can use one jig on both.

I'm touting this for T-laps and cross laps, but you can use it for end laps as well. To do so, add a fifth scrap as a positioning block. Attach it to the underside of the secondary platform so the workpiece end can butt against it.

Complete the platform by mounting the secondary platform. Use the mating workpiece as a gauge to position and align this small platform. Make sure the gauge workpiece is captured snugly between the main and secondary platforms, then screw the secondary platform to the fences.

LAPPING WITH A DADO CUTTER

The dado head offers a fast, single-setup approach to cutting laps. In effect, this is the same cut I make on the router table with the mortising bit and my T-square sled. The difference is that the dado cutter is rotating on an axis that's at right angles to the router bit.

On the router table, you need backup behind the work to prevent tearout, while on the table saw, you don't.

You could mount a long auxiliary facing to the miter gauge, then attach a stop to it, out to the right of the cutter. Or, you could clamp a standoff block to the rip fence and use your standard miter gauge.

The latter is a common technique. The fence position determines how far from the end of the workpiece the shoulder will be. But instead of having the workpiece end in contact with the fence throughout the shoulder cut, you offset the fence by the thickness of the standoff block.

The cutting routine for an end lap, then, is to lay the workpiece in the miter gauge, and slide the end against the standoff block. Hold the work tight to the miter gauge and feed it across the dado cutter, cutting a dado that's half the stock's thickness in depth and as wide as your dado cutter will cut (usually $^{13}/_{16}$"). The shoulder is formed right where you want it, but there's still waste between the cut and the end of the workpiece. Back the work about $^3/_4$" to the left for a second pass, and, if necessary, again for a third pass to complete the lap.

This routine works even for cross laps. Your saw's rip fence, after all, can be moved a couple of feet at least, and possibly as many as 4', to the right of the blade. This enables you to use the method to accurately, uniformly and consistently locate laps that are relatively far from the end of a piece.

The trick is in having the same control over the cut width. Alternatives include laying out the margins of each

Use a miter gauge to guide the work when using a dado head to cut an end lap. Clamp a standoff block to the rip fence and use it to locate the workpiece for the shoulder cut. Then shift the work to the left for second and subsequent passes as you waste the full width of the lap.

The fence must be set farther from the cutter to waste a cross lap. Since a cross lap has two shoulders, cobble together a two-step standoff block. The far step is for the left shoulder, the near step for the right shoulder. Stack scraps of the appropriate thickness together to produce the width of cut needed and clamp them to the fence with one clamp.

lap and cutting to the marks.

A fixture-oriented approach entails using a spacer equal in thickness to the difference between the lap width and the cut width. (For example, if the lap is to be $1^3/_4$" wide and you are using a dado cutter set up at $^3/_4$", the spacer must be 1" thick.) The cutting routine

would be to butt the work against the standoff block and cut the left shoulder of the lap. Then insert the spacer between the work and the standoff block, and cut the right shoulder. Any remaining waste is removed with a cut that you merely eyeball.

Cut the lap with a mortising bit that has a shank-mounted pilot bearing. With the bearing trapped between the platforms, the bit produces a smooth, square-shouldered cut that perfectly matches the width of the gauge workpiece. The fences are cut as well as the work, but they back up the good material so splintering at the outfeed edge of the cut is eliminated.

Sawing Half Laps

Not everyone is as enamored of router woodworking as I am. Saws like the band saw, the table saw, the radial-arm saw, the sliding compound miter saw, and yes, even the carpenter's work-horse, the circular saw, all are capable of roughing out half laps.

Doing the job with a circular saw or sliding compound miter saw is a wasting process. You adjust the saw's cut depth to half the stock thickness, carefully kerf the margin(s), then waste the material between the margins with multitudes of kerfs. Typically, a ragged cheek results. It has to be smoothed to glue well. But if you're using a circular saw, you are probably doing something rough, where nails or screws work as well as glue.

The band saw roughs out end laps very quickly but leaves you with a rough surface that needs to be flattened and smoothed to glue well. Some woodworkers opt to rough out half laps on the band saw, then finish them with a router. To me, that's extra setups, extra work. Besides, you'll be hard-pressed to effectively band-saw a lap that isn't at the end of a workpiece.

The radial-arm saw is a very effective tool for making half laps. Set up with a dado head, a well-tuned radial-arm saw will cut end and cross laps quickly and cleanly. You can see layout lines, so locating the cut precisely is easy. You can do angled laps easily; just swing the arm right or left for the cut. You can set stops to expedite production jobs.

The saw that gives you some options is the table saw. You can use your everyday saw blade or a dado head. Guide the work with the miter gauge, a cutoff box or a tenoning jig.

You can waste the occasional lap on a sliding compound miter saw. Lay out the lap's shoulders on the work. Adjust the saw to limit the cut depth. Saw inside the shoulder marks to clearly delineate the extent of the area to be wasted, then kerf, kerf, kerf, progressively removing all the waste. To get a flat cheek, you must bump the work away from the fence with a spacer (the low strip visible behind the workpiece).

LAPPING WITH A TENONING JIG

A tenoning jig is a good alternative if you don't have a dado head or you don't want to switch from blade to dado set. With a tenoning jig, you can use the blade to cut the laps. This is a two-setup approach in which you saw the cheeks using the tenoning jig, then cut the shoulders using the miter gauge.

The cut depth for both the cheek cut and the shoulder cut are critical. Cut too deep and the kerf will show on the edges of the assembled frame. If you cut the cheek you can correct it with the shoulder cut.

Use whatever tenoning jig you have for the cheek cut. Delta's block-of-iron model is great, but I don't think it works any better than the shop-made fence-rider I use (see the Mortise-and-Tenon Joint chapter for a plan). Mount the jig on the saw and position it for the cut, adjust the blade height and saw the cheeks, one after the other.

Assembly

It's not difficult to assemble a frame joined with half laps. You must apply clamps to the individual joints, however, in addition to using clamps that draw the assembly together. Use bar or pipe clamps to pull the joints tight at the shoulders. Then squeeze the cheeks of individual joints tight using C-clamps or spring clamps.

A table-saw tenoning jig, whether purchased or shop-made, will cut the cheeks of end laps with the blade that's installed in your table saw. Elevate the blade to the full length of the lap, and set the jig to properly position the cheek. Cut through the workpiece.

Make the shoulder cuts with the miter gauge. If you are in a production mode, with a dozen or more to saw, use a standoff block clamped to the rip fence to position the shoulders uniformly. Bump the end of the workpiece against the block, then feed the piece across the blade. The offset between the end of the workpiece and the rip fence prevents the waste from being wedged between the fence and blade, which leads to kickback.

Gluing up a half-lapped frame requires the usual compliment of pipe or bar clamps to pull the shoulders of the joints tight. Each joint also requires a C-clamp or spring clamp to pinch its cheeks tight together.

MORTISE-AND-TENON JOINTS

I may be a power tool kind-o'-guy, but I nevertheless favor traditional joints, those proven through centuries of use. The mortise and tenon is one. It has been in use not simply for hundreds of years, but for thousands of years, with examples found in ancient Egyptian furniture.

The mortise and tenon is a first-rate joint for frames of all sorts, and for post-and-apron and post-and-rail constructions. In other words, you can (and should) use it for cabinet doors; for face, web and other types of frames; for connecting aprons to legs in desks, tables and chairs; and to join rails to posts in chests and cabinets, in beds, workbenches and worktables.

ROUTING TENONS

A good tenon has straight, square shoulders and smooth cheeks. Smooth surfaces glue best, so you want your tenons to have smooth cheeks. Gaps and misalignments at the shoulder not only degrade the joint's appearance, they weaken it. You want a clean and square intersection of the shoulder and the cheek — no ridges of waste, which could prevent the joint from closing completely. The shoulders also must be in the same plane all the way around the workpiece, so they seat tight against the mortise's shoulders.

Router-cut tenons meet these criteria, and they are easy to make. A variety of ways exist to cut tenons with a router that all yield similar results.

What you're going to find, as you read the next few paragraphs, is that the cutting tenons with a router is almost exactly like cutting end laps with a router.

If you prefer to work with a portable router, you can use the right-angle platform, presented in the Sliding Dovetail Joint chapter. It does a great job on tenons with two cheeks and shoulder across the faces but not the edges. I think you can work out how to set it up and cut tenons, using the info in the sliding dovetail chapter and the Half-Lap Joints chapter.

If you have a router table, you can produce tenons with a long bit. Stand the rail on edge and feed it along the fence. A pass on each face and edge will produce a clean tenon. Again, you'll find info on this basic operation in the Lap Joints chapter.

ROUTER TABLE SLED

My favorite tenoning approach depends on the lapping sled I presented in the Half-Lap Joints chapter. You use the same mortising bit for tenoning that you use for lapping. With the jig and bit, you can set up in two or three minutes, you don't have any layout to

I use this beefy T-square on the router table for routing tenons. The self-clamping stop fits over the sled's fence to position the work for cuts. Cutting a tenon takes only one pass per cheek. Lay the work on the table, pull it against the sled's fence and stop and feed it across the bit. The bit cuts cheek and shoulder simultaneously.

For cutting tenons, I use mortising bits. How's that for confusing! The bits are designed to clear smooth, wide recesses such as hinge mortises. They do a great job on laps and tenons as well. Many sizes are available.

do and you can cut a typical tenon in four quick passes.

Here is how I set up, then cut a tenon.

The first thing, of course, is to install the bit in the router and set its elevation. Use a rule to measure the exposure of the cutting edge above the table. I set the bit a skosh under the width of the mortise's shoulder; that way I can creep up on the just-right setting via test cuts. (The just-right setting is determined by fitting a test tenon in a mortise.)

Set up the sled next. You must set the stop on the sled's fence to establish the tenon length. To do this, measure from the cut made into the fence by the bit. (You always want to use the same bit with the sled; otherwise you will get tear-out at the shoulders.) If the tenon is to be 1" long, for example, align the 1" mark on the rule at the edge of the cut. Slip the stop onto the fence and bring it against the end of the rule. Seat it firmly so it is square both to the fence and the tabletop. Tighten its clamp.

Now cut a sample tenon to prove the setup. Make a pass, cutting the first cheek and shoulder. Roll the workpiece over. Make a pass, cutting the second cheek and shoulder.

Check the fit of this tenon in your mortise. You need a close fit for the joint to glue well. If you have to hammer on the tenon to close the joint, the fit is too close. Hand pressure should close it. On the other hand, the joint should stay closed until you separate the parts.

To refine the fit, raise or lower the bit. Cut another test tenon and fit it to the mortise. When you have the settings right, cut the real work.

You can set the bit height using a rule or an actual mortise. Leave the bit a skosh low and cut a test tenon to fit to a mortise. Fine-tune the bit height based on the fit.

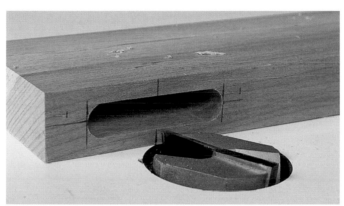

Position the stop by measuring from the shoulder of the cut in the sled's fence. Always use the same bit for tenoning, so the shoulder cut remains accurate for setups and for backing up the tenon shoulders.

Fitting Tenon to Mortise

Obviously, plain "vanilla" tenons, which have the same width of shoulder all around, are the easiest to cut. An offset tenon or one with wider or narrower edge shoulders requires more setups.

In any case, though, your square-cornered tenon doesn't match your routed mortise, with its rounded ends. You can resolve this problem in one of several ways. Some address it by squaring the ends of the mortise with a chisel. I've often filed the tenon's corners to roughly match the mortise.

A third option is to scale the tenon width so the square-cornered tenon fits the round-ended mortise. The primary glue surfaces are the broad cheeks, and you have the shoulders working to resist twisting and racking. If the narrow edges of the tenon aren't in contact with the ends of the mortise, it doesn't significantly impact the strength of the joint.

Fitting integral tenons to routed mortises typically involves hand work — rounding off the corners. You can pare the corners with a chisel, done here, or soften them with a file or sandpaper.

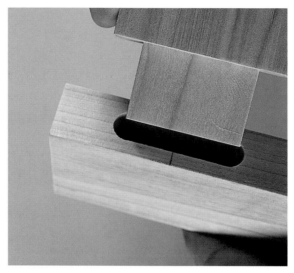

The corners of a tenon don't necessarily have to be rounded off to fit a routed mortise. It is faster to adjust the tenon width to fit the mortise, eliminating the handwork. The dominant strength comes from the joint bond between tenon cheeks and mortise cheeks. The tenon shoulders conceal the mortise.

It may be heresy, but I don't think the edges of the tenon need to fit tightly to the ends of the mortise. Lots of craftsmen worry about the hydraulics in gluing a tightly fitted mortise and tenon. As you can see, this joint has smooth cheeks on both mortise and tenon for an ideal glue bond, but it also has reservoirs for excess glue along the ends and bottom.

Loose-Tenon Joinery

A mortise-and-loose-tenon joint is created by cutting mortises into both
mating parts and using a separate strip
as a tenon to link them. With a horizontal borer, this type of joint is a
cinch to make. But the horizontal
borer is not a commonplace piece of
shop equipment. With a hollow-chisel
mortiser, it's a real challenge because
this tool isn't specifically designed to
make end mortises.

My approach hinges on the use of
my mortising block. The typical fixture
— like the Q&D — enables you to
rout edge mortises but not end mortises. The mortising block enables both.

Switching from edge mortising to
end mortising requires only a workholder swap. When I'm doing rails and
stiles — making doors or web frames,
for example — I'll rout all the edge
mortises in the stiles, then switch work
holders and do the end mortises.

Swapping work rests entails backing
out a pair of mounting bolts. Nothing
in the setup changes, so your end mortise will duplicate the edge mortises.

End mortises involve no alignment
per se. Tucking the work against the
rest aligns it for the cut. The rubber
tips of the toggle clamps I have allow
the work to deflect when the bit
plunges against it. As a consequence, I
use a deep throat clamp or two to secure the work to the jig for end mortises. Yes, it does slow down changeover,
but it's secure.

With the mortises routed, making
loose tenons is a matter of resawing
and planing strips of suitable stock to
fit the mortises. Rip the stock to width,
round the edges on the router table,
then crosscut individual tenons.

Loose-tenon joints are not as fast as
biscuits or pocket screws, but a whole
lot more satisfying to me as a woodworker.

Loose-tenon joinery is a modern variation on traditional mortise-and-tenon joinery. You cut
mortises into both mating parts and use a separate strip as a tenon to link them. A single
mortising-block setup serves for routing both edge and end mortises, saving setup time.
Fitting loose tenons is easier than fitting integral tenons, again saving time, but also producing stronger joints.

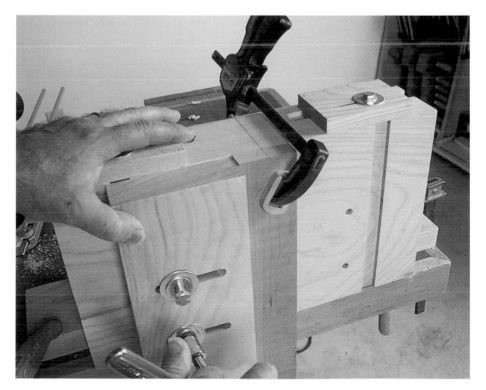

Changing over the mortising block from edge mortises to end mortises is a matter of removing the horizontal work rest and replacing it with the vertical one. Clamp a rail to the
jig with its mortise center line aligned with the jig's setup line to locate the work rest while
you secure it. Nothing else about the setup changes.

The rubber tips of toggle clamps have too much give, so I use a deep-throat clamp or two to secure the work for end mortising. The lower clamp bears on a rabbeted scrap that extends the clamp's reach while countering the tendency of the other clamp to pull the workpiece away from the face of the block.

The finished joint, ready for assembly, has identical mortises.

REINFORCING COPE-AND-STICK JOINTS

A loose tenon — though small in section — greatly strengthens a commonplace cope-and-stick joint. Rout the mortises first, then rout the copes and do the sticking cuts. Here, the loose tenon is centered on the stock to facilitate mortising and assembly. Though it doesn't align with the stub tenon produced by the coping cut, this misalignment doesn't show in the assembled joint.

MAKING LOOSE TENONS

The common way to produce the loose tenons is to mill strips of stock to the appropriate thickness. Rip the strips to width, then round the edges with a round-over or small half-round bit. Crosscut the individual tenons. Some craftsmen rout grooves in their tenons to provide a reservoir for excess glue; I don't bother with this extra step.

I usually use scraps of the working stock to produce the tenons, but you don't have to use scraps or the same wood. On occasion, I'll find and use leftover tenon strips on a project.

You can save a step, and in the bargain provide yourself with a little assembly flexibility, if you make the tenons square-edged. Simply cut the strips a little less wide, so they'll slide into the mortises.

The critical gluing surfaces are the cheeks, not the edges. Eliminating the edges that so nicely fit the rounded-end mortises doesn't degrade the strength of the joint appreciably. It does, however, provide that reservoir for the excess glue, and in addition, allows you to adjust the joint slightly as you assemble it.

TWINS

Building a mortising block with wide edge-guide tracks allows you to use the fixture for routing twin mortises. A spacer shares the channel with the edge-guide facing. With the spacer between the block and the facing, the router is positioned to do the first mortise. Moving the spacer behind the edge-guide facing bumps the router out, aligning it to rout the second mortise.

In post-and-rail constructions where the stock is thicker than more commonplace frames, you can make stronger joints using twin mortises. The inner mortises intersect, so the tenons in them are mitered. The outer mortises can be deeper.

BISCUITRY

Biscuit joinery is so fast and easy it almost seems like cheating. And boy, I have tell you, I'm no cheater. Consequently, I pretty much ignored the system, sticking with more traditional joinery even when I worked with sheet goods.

A few years ago, I was introduced to a novel (to me, anyway) post-and-panel construction. The posts and rails were joined with loose tenons, and flat, veneered medium-density fiberboard panels were joined to the posts and rails with biscuits. The whole point of this construction is to reduce production cost by reducing the labor.

Since then, I've used biscuit joinery to build tool chests, a router table, bookcases, wall cabinets, and a lot of other furniture. All are pieces built primarily of plywood, and I had to complete all of them without sacrificing strength or appearance.

Speed and economy are the whole point of biscuit joinery.

The biscuit joiner is a single-purpose tool, invented in the 1950's to cut a joint that didn't exist. It was designed specifically to make strong joints very quickly in manmade sheet materials, such as plywood, MDF and melamine.

Biscuitry Basics

For the uninitiated, a biscuit joint is a butt joint splined with a small beech wafer, called the biscuit. Simple in appearance, biscuits are fairly sophisticated. Shaped like tiny, flattened footballs, they're stamped out, a process that compresses them. Add moisture and they swell up.

The linchpin of the biscuiting process is a dedicated portable power tool known as a biscuit joiner. The tool enables you to plunge a cutter into your workpiece to make a slot that will, unsurprisingly, accommodate a biscuit. Well, half a biscuit.

To make a simple biscuit joint, you cut a slot into each mating surface, insert a biscuit into one slot, then slide the mating part into position. As you close the joint, the protruding biscuit half penetrates the second slot, providing a mechanical connection.

At this point the reason biscuits are compressed becomes clear. When you use ordinary white or yellow glue, the moisture in the glue prompts the biscuit to swell, and the biscuit locks itself in the matching slots, strengthening the joint. (If you use polyurethane glue or an epoxy, you should dampen a biscuit as you insert it in its slot.)

The result is a joint that's easy to produce, invisible and surprisingly strong. Biscuits can be used to reinforce — to spline, in effect — almost any butted joint. One qualification: The contact surface between the mating parts must be thick enough and wide enough to accommodate one of the three common biscuits, which are #0 (the smallest), #10 and #20 (the largest). The most common biscuit joints use multiples, arraying them in a line across a wide joint or stacking them in thick stock.

Biscuits are most appropriate, in my opinion, in casework produced from sheet goods: plywood, melamine, veneered MDF and the like. Often, sheet

The biscuit is engineered to swell and seize in the mating slots when dampened with a water-based glue. Just a quick dip in water, and the grid and other markings pressed into the biscuit's face disappear.

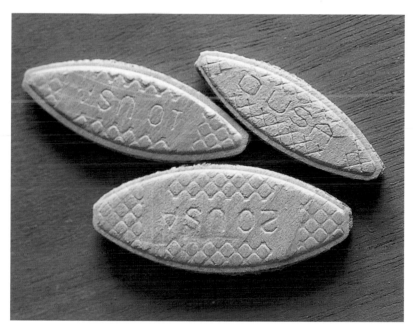

Biscuits are made in several sizes. The three most common — simply because all biscuit joiners can produce slots for them — are the #20 (largest), the #10 and the #0 (smallest).

goods are selected for a project to circumvent lumber prep and panel glue-ups, to shorten the production time in other words. So a joinery that also shortens production time — without sacrificing strength and accuracy — is appropriate.

Layout and Slot-Cutting Tips

Many of the benefits of biscuit joinery as a process derive from the tool used. It has only one purpose — cutting slots for biscuits — so it's always set up for operation, and there are no bit changes, no jig setups and usually no cutter adjustments. Once in a while you may adjust the machine for a different biscuit size. This involves nothing more than a twist of a small knob to change how deep the cutter plunges into the work.

The tool has two reference surfaces: the base and the fence. Every joiner is designed to locate the center of the slot $\frac{3}{8}$" from the base, which centers the slot on the edge of $\frac{3}{4}$" stock. There are registration marks delineating the vertical center line of the slot on the tool's nose, its underside and its fence.

Fence designs vary from model to model. Some are easily and precisely adjustable and others are not. You should be able to adjust the angle of the fence and its elevation above the blade. Just bear in mind that not all fences are perfectly aligned with the cutter and not all will stay locked.

Rule number one is to always use the same reference surface for slotting both parts of any joint. On the tool, I think your first choice should be the base, simply because the machine design virtually guarantees it to be accurate. It's easy to hold the tool steady when it's resting solidly, squarely on its base, less so when it's hanging from the fence. Keep in mind, too, that the nose of the biscuit joiner must be square to the surface being slotted. If the slot isn't cut square to the surface, the joint won't line up.

If you have to shift the location of the slot, use a shim under either the tool or the work. You'll find, as I have, that you can orient the work and the tool so you can use the base as the reference to produce slots for any form of biscuit joint.

The base is a reliable, stable reference surface. The distance between the base and the cutter never changes; it can't creep out of adjustment. Moreover, you are least likely to rock the tool when it's resting on its base and both of your hands are gripping it.

Many users favor the fence as the reference surface because it can be adjusted to accommodate different stock thicknesses or to locate a slot off center. Because it's so easy to inadvertently tilt the tool when registering the cut with the fence, I tend to hold the fence against the work with one hand while operating the tool with the other.

On the workpieces, use the surface that must line up in the final assembly as references. For example, you need the top surface of a case top to be flush with the top edge of the case side, and you want to use the biscuit joiner's base as the reference. To do so, slot the top with its top surface down on the bench top, and slot the side with the joiner's base flush with the side's top edge.

How do you accomplish the latter? One good way is to butt the side's end against a "fence" held in a bench vise. Stand the joiner on its nose, base against the fence and make the cut.

Layout couldn't be simpler. Place the parts together, just the way you want them in the assembled joint. Tick across the seam to mark the center of each biscuit slot on the mating pieces. Align the joiner's registration mark on the tick to cut the slot. Typically, that's all the layout that's necessary. Occasionally, you have to extend the tick across an edge or onto a face so it's visible when the joiner is in position to cut a slot. You don't need to address the slot's vertical position because that's determined by the tool's fence or base.

In a wide joint — joining a bottom to a side in a 2'-deep cabinet, for example — you need to use several biscuits. The rule of thumb is to space biscuits 6" to 8" apart on center. Offset the end ones about 3" from the edge of the workpiece. You can do this by measurement, or you can simply eyeball the locations.

Stacking slots is common when the thickness of the working stock exceeds 1". If your material is a uniform thickness, you can cut a slot, then roll the piece over and cut the second. The hazard here is the odd piece that's thicker or thinner than its mates. The sure approach is to use that shim under the joiner base to elevate it when cutting the second slot.

When stock thickness tops 1", you should stack biscuits. You can clamp the workpiece to the bench and cut the lower slot, then raise the joiner with a shim and cut the upper one. In bulkier frame stock, you can stack three biscuits.

An Edge-to-Edge Glueup

Biscuits in edge-to-edge joints are primarily alignment aids. As such, relatively few of them will do the trick. Spacing them closer than 6" on center is overkill — extra work with no benefit.

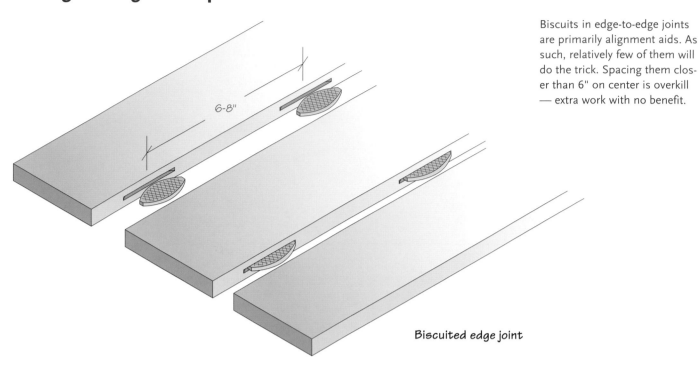

6-8"

Biscuited edge joint

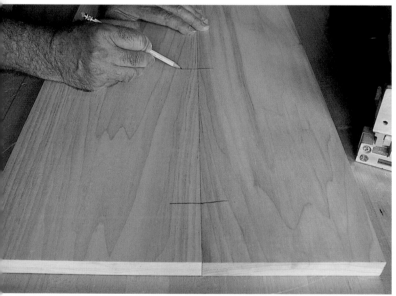

Biscuits offer a fast, reliable system for aligning the boards in an edge-to-edge assembly. Butt the mating boards and slash across the seam between them every 6" or so (above). You *can* lay out the marks with a tape, but there's no reason for anything other than a guesstimated layout. You can situate the slashes any way, at any angle, curve or other, because you'll only reference the joiner right at the edge. The slots you cut in the mating edges will align (right).

Casework

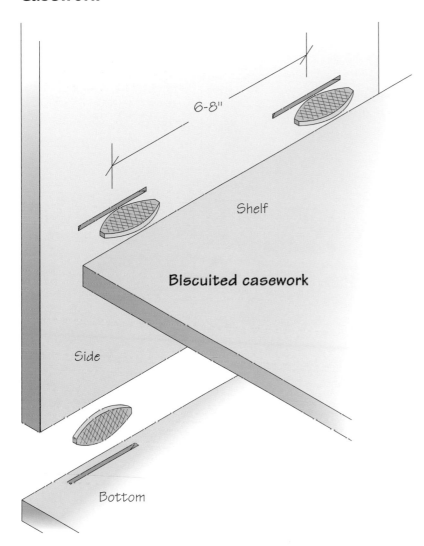

6-8"

Shelf

Biscuited casework

Side

Bottom

Case construction of manufactured materials such as plywood, MDF and melamine is what biscuit joinery was invented for. With biscuitry, all joints are in effect butt joints. Parts are easy to dimension, and the required slots are easy to lay out and cut.

For a simple case like a wall cabinet with two sides, a top and a bottom, and two or three shelves, mock up the assembly and mark slot locations on sides and shelves at the same time. Square up a shelf in position, as shown, and mark the center of the mating slots on the face of the side and the shelf.

For a large unit or multiple assemblies, you can lay out edge slot locations on a stack of like parts. Use a square and extend the lines across the edge of the stack. Then extend the line onto the faces so you will have a visible reference for the joiner.

Free both hands for the biscuit joiner by clamping a block to your bench and butting the part against it. After cutting the slots in one edge, simply spin the workpiece 180° and you're ready to slot the opposite edge. Clamp handling is eliminated; production is accelerated.

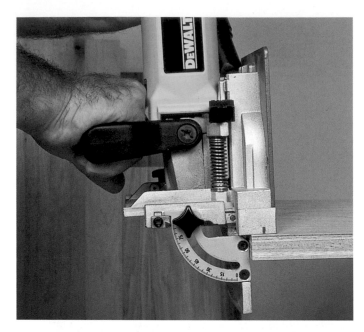

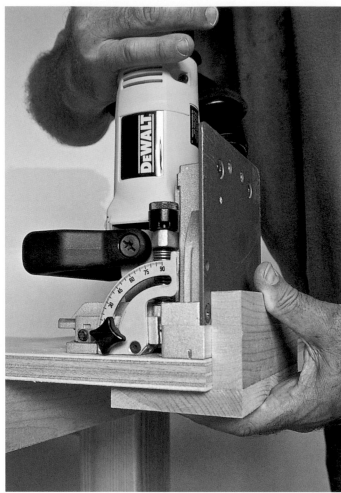

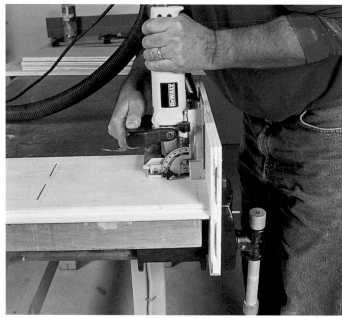

You can align the biscuit joiner in several ways for a face cut at the end of a panel. You can use the tool's fence (top left), but plunging the tool when it's overhanging the edge is likely to rock it, so this isn't my favorite option. Better is make a jig to hold at the end of the panel so the joiner base can reference it (above). This puts the nose of the tool square on the panel, making it more stable during the plunge cut. A third option is to grip a vertical reference piece in a bench vise, then butt the panel to be slotted against it and clamp it (left). This allows you to grip the tool with both hands.

Clamp a fence across a case part to position the joiner for cutting face slots. Mark the line of intersection between the parts — for example, a shelf and a case side — and plant your fence on the line. Stand the joiner on its nose, its base against the fence, and cut the face slots. In some situations, the fence can be the actual mating part. Stand the part in place, mark slot locations on it and its mate, then lay it flat and clamp the two parts. Rest the joiner on the flat to cut the edge slots; stand it on its nose, base against the fence, to cut the face slots.

STEP-OFF GAUGE

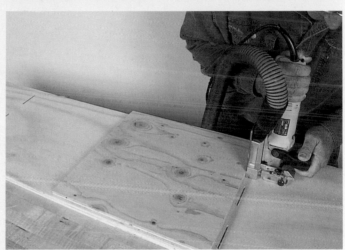

A step-off gauge is a time-saving jig that helps locate and cut repetitive slots in casework. The length of the gauge equals the distance from the bottom of one shelf to the bottom of the next. Cut face slots across its bottom edge, and use biscuits (without glue, of course) to mate it to the first row of slots in a case side. The top edge of the gauge becomes a fence and a layout guide for cutting the second row of slots. Step the gauge to mate its biscuits into the newly cut slots, and again, use it as a fence to cut the third row of slots.

The board is especially useful when you're crafting a set of bookcases, or any other project that requires making multiple sides and cutting rows of slots a uniform distance apart. But it can be helpful just ensuring that rows of slots in a pair of case sides line up. If the spacing between shelves is not uniform, you can begin with the widest spacing, then cut down the gauge in stages as you progress to the narrowest spacing.

Miters

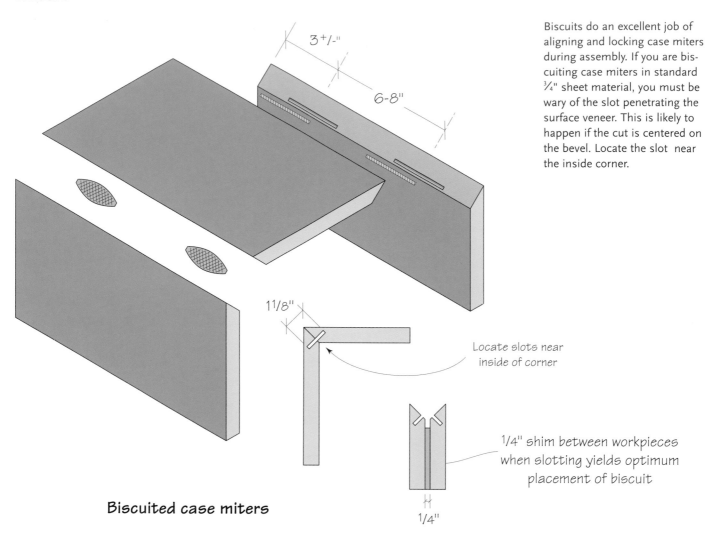

Biscuits do an excellent job of aligning and locking case miters during assembly. If you are biscuiting case miters in standard ¾" sheet material, you must be wary of the slot penetrating the surface veneer. This is likely to happen if the cut is centered on the bevel. Locate the slot near the inside corner.

3 +/- "

6-8"

11/8"

Locate slots near inside of corner

Biscuited case miters

¼" shim between workpieces when slotting yields optimum placement of biscuit

1/4"

Clamp the inside faces of beveled case parts together so you can use the base as the reference for slotting the bevels. With the parts lined up carefully, the bevels form a 90° cradle to support the base. If you use a ¼"-thick spacer between the parts, you'll get the best placement of the slots. Alternatively, you can use the joiner fence to guide the cuts on individual case parts.

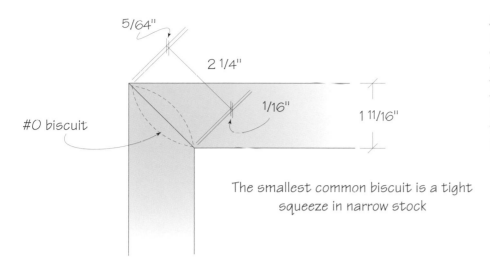

5/64"

2 1/4"

1/16"

1 11/16"

#0 biscuit

The smallest common biscuit is a tight
squeeze in narrow stock

A biscuit is a practical way to spline a frame miter. Even when the mitered edge barely exceeds the length of the biscuit slot, you can be confident the slot won't break through the frame at the tip. But if you plan to mold an edge of the assembled frame, it's a good idea to shift the biscuit away from that edge so the profile cut doesn't expose the biscuit.

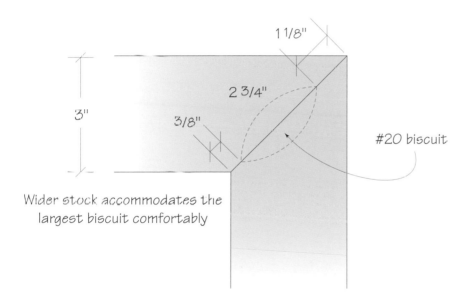

1 1/8"

2 3/4"

3"

3/8"

#20 biscuit

Wider stock accommodates the
largest biscuit comfortably

Biscuited frame miters

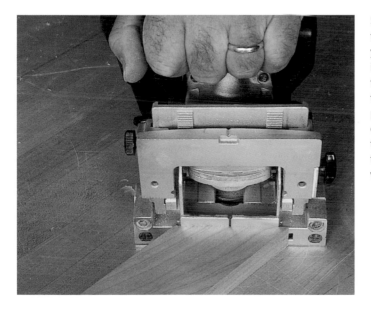

Securely clamp any frame part to prevent it from moving as you plunge the cutter. This cut is particularly dicey because the tool's antislippage pins are off the surface to be cut and can't provide any traction. It is especially easy, in this situation, for the tool to jump to the side as the cutting teeth contact the wood.

Face-Frame Joinery

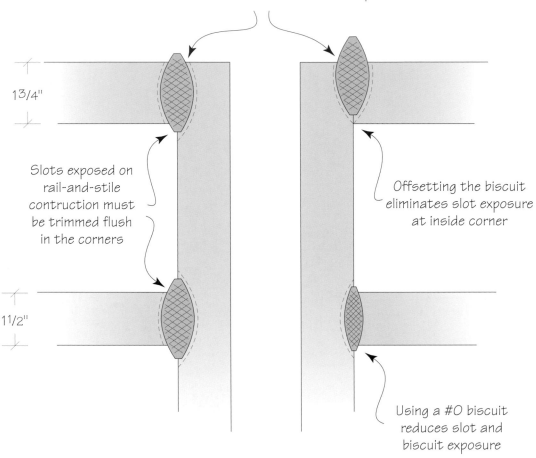

Biscuit exposure on the top edge is often up and out of sight or concealed beneath a countertop

13/4"

Slots exposed on rail-and-stile contruction must be trimmed flush in the corners

11/2"

Offsetting the biscuit eliminates slot exposure at inside corner

Using a #0 biscuit reduces slot and biscuit exposure

Biscuits do a good job of joining the parts of a face frame, but there is a cosmetic issue. The slot for even the small, #0 biscuit is longer than 2". In many instances, face frame rails aren't that wide. Assemble the frame and the ends of the slots are visible. A common view is that the slot exposure is no big deal, since it'll only be visible when doors and drawers are open. The situation is different if the frame is for a bookcase, with the inner edges of the frame exposed. Because the frame is fixed to the case, strong joints in the frame itself aren't essential.

Biscuits in face frames

If you opt to biscuit a face frame, lay out the parts in a mock assembly to mark the slot locations. Lay a biscuit on the seam between rail and stile to determine what size biscuit to use and what, if any, offset is appropriate.

If the top and bottom edges of the face frame won't be visible, you can offset the slot. There's no exposure at the inside corners, but as much as half the biscuit will protrude at the outside edge. After the glue sets, trim it flush.

FACE FRAME TO CASE ALIGNMENT

Like an edge-to-edge joint between well-jointed boards with the proper glue application, a glued edge-to-face joint — such as that joins a face frame to a case — is strong and without need of reinforcement. But a few biscuits placed in key spots guarantees your face frame will be aligned just the way you want it. They prevent the frame from squirrming out of position as you apply clamps.

Set the assembled frame on the assembled case and mark slot locations. You don't need a lot of biscuits, and you don't necessarily need them in all edges. Two or three biscuits in each side and one at the center of the top is sufficient for alignment in all but the biggest units.

Use the joiner's base as the reference when cutting slots in a case and face frame. Here, the case is on its side. I'll upend it to cut the slot in the top, so the reference surface is consistent.

Stand the face frame on edge to slot it for mounting to the case. If I wanted a ¼" overhang along this edge, I would place a scrap of ¼" MDF under the joiner base.

With the slots cut and the biscuits in place, you can drop the frame onto the case and know it is aligned just the way you want it.

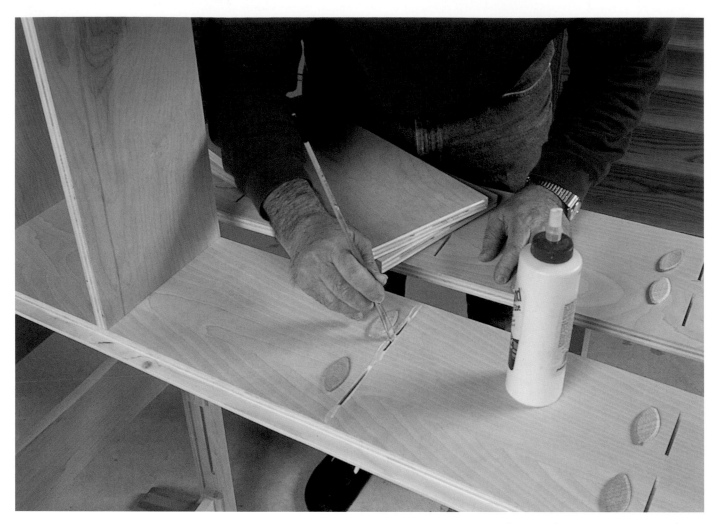

Assembly

In assembling a biscuit joint, it's essential to get enough glue in the mating slots and on the biscuit to promote expansion of the little wafer. But be discrete; you don't want it welling out of the slots, dripping and gushing across the nice wood. Experience makes it easier.

You can buy applicators designed for biscuit slots. I usually run the glue-bottle tip along the edge of the slot, then use an artist's brush to spread it through the slot. I run a bead from slot to slot, and I use the brush to spread it too. When the glue is applied to both mating parts, I stuff a biscuit in each slot and close the joint. Seat it firmly, and move on to the next.

Be wary of seating biscuits one at a time, and of trying to apply glue to all the joints in an assembly before closing any of them. The biscuits can swell and make assembly difficult.

A benefit of biscuit joinery is that your case will clamp up square. (This assumes, of course, that all your parts are squarely cut.) The scramble to wrench the case into proper alignment before the glue sets up is reduced to a low-key measuring of diagonals to confirm what you already know.

In a large, multijoint construction, apply glue and assemble the joints one by one. Biscuits start swelling as soon as they are dampened with glue. I sweep glue through each slot in a row with a small brush, then insert the biscuits and set the mating part in place.

SUPPLIERS

AMANA TOOL
120 Carolyn Boulevard
Farmingdale, NY 11735
800-445-0077
www.amanatool.com
High quality saw blades, router bits, and shaper cutters. Sells through dealers.

BENCH DOG
3310 Fifth Street NE
Minneapolis, MN 55418
800-786-8902
www.benchdog.com
Router tables, router lifts, and associated products.

FREUD TOOLS
218 Feld Avenue
High Point, NC 27263
800-334-4107
www.freudtools.com
High quality saw blades, router bits, and shaper cutters. Sells through dealers.

HIGHLAND HARDWARE
1045 North Highland Avenue NE
Atlanta, GA 30306
800-241-6748
www.highlandhardware.com
Retailer of tools, accessories, and supplies.

INFINITY CUTTING TOOLS
2762 Summerdale Drive
Clearwater, FL 33761
877-872-2487
www.infinitytools.com
High quality saw blades, router bits, and shaper cutters. Sells direct.

LEE VALLEY
U.S.:
P.O. Box 1780
Ogdensburg, NY 13669-6780
800-267-8735
Canada:
P.O. Box 6295, Station J
Ottawa, ON K2A 1T4
800-267-8761
www.leevalley.com
Woodworking tool manufacturer (Veritas) and supercatalog retailer of tools, accessories, supplies, and hardware.

MICROFENCE
13160 Saticoy Street
North Hollywood, CA 91605
818 982 4367
www.microfence.com
Finest router edge guide (and kindred accessories) known to woodworking

REID TOOL SUPPLY
2265 Black Creek Road
Muskegon, MI 49441
800-253-0421
www.reidtool.com
Extensive catalog of machinist's tools, hardware, and fascinating widgets. First place to look for toggle clamps, plastic knobs, and other jig-making hardware.

ROCKLER WOODWORKING AND HARDWARE
4365 Willow Drive
Medina, MN 55340
800-279-4441
www.rockler.com
Supercatalog retailer of tools, accessories, supplies, and hardware.

PAT WARNER
1427 Kenora Street
Escondido CA 92027-3940
www.patwarner.com
High quality router accessories, jigs and fixtures, and sound router-woodworking information.

WOODLINE USA
www.woodline.com
Extensive catalog of affordable router bits and shaper cutters. Sells direct.

WOODCENTRAL
www.woodcentral.com
Woodworking forum—discussion boards, project gallery, book and tool reviews, article archive and lots more.

WOODHAVEN
501 West First Avenue
Durant, IA 52747-9729
800-344-6657
www.woodhaven.com
Router tables, woodworking jigs and fixtures, router bits, and more.

INDEX

Angle sled, 41

Beaded joint, 17
Bevels, 42, 43, 54–57
Biscuit joinery, 114
  assembly, 126
  casework, 119–120
  edge-to-edge glueup, 118
  face-frame joinery, 124–125
  layout and slot-cutting, 116–117
  miters, 122–123
  uses for, 9
Blind cut, 23
Blind dado joint, 19, 23, 25, 26, 29
Blind rabbets, 37–38
Butted edge joint, 9

Casework, 119–120
Clamps, 10, 27, 29, 46–47
Cope-and-stick joints, 112
Crosscut sled
  dado joints, 20, 22, 23, 25
  half-lap joints, 86
  miter joints, 41
  rabbet joints, 35
Cutting frame miter joints, 44–45

Dado cutter, 12, 90
Dado joints, 18–19
  advanced, 20
  blind dado, 19, 23, 25, 26, 29
  cutting dadoes, 19–20
  rabbet joints, 31–32
  router, 24–28
  stopped dado, 19, 23, 25, 26, 29
  table saw, 20–23
  through dado, 19
Dovetail joints, 72. *See also* Sliding
  dovetail joints
  fine-tuning the setup, 78–79
  half-blind dovetail jig, 73–80
  mounting the jig, 75
  organizing the parts, 80
  router, 73–80

Edge joints, 8–9
  assembly, 10
  cutting the joint, 11
  router, 14–16
  table saw, 12–13
  tongue-and-groove, 11–17
  tongue-and-groove cutters, 17
Edge-to-edge joinery, 9
  biscuits, 118
  tongue-and-groove, 11–17

Face-frame joinery, 124–125
Fence
  acute-angle, 55–56

biscuit and slot-cutting,
  116–117
  obtuse-angle, 57
  rip fence, 21, 40
  sacrificial rip fence facing, 13
  twin-fence guide, 64–65
Frame miters, 44–45, 123

Groove, 18, 19, 29, 52–57

Half-lap joints, 81
  dado cutter, 90
  router, 83–89
  table saw, 91–92
  tenoning jig, 92
Hollow-chisel mortiser, 95

Jointer-cut rabbets, 35

Keying flat miters, 48-49

Lap joinery, 82. *See also* Half-lap
  joints
Lapping sled, 108–109

Metric conversion chart, 2
Miter gauge, 20, 41, 90, 92
Miter joints, 39
  assembly, 46–47
  bevels, 43
  biscuits, 122–123
  cutting case, 40–42
  frame miters, 44–45, 123
  keying flat miters, 48-49
  table saw, 40–41, 44–45
Miter sled, 44–45
Mortise-and-tenon joints, 93
  cope-and-stick joints, 112
  cutting tenons, 104–109
  design, 94–97
  fitting, 94–97, 110
  loose-tenon joinery, 111–113
  Q&D fixture setup, 103
  router, 98–103, 108–109
  router free, 95-97
  setting up, 100–102
  table saw, 104–107
  twins, 113

Q&D fixture, 103

Rabbet joints, 30
  blind cuts, 37–38
  jointer, 35
  router, 36–38
  stopped cuts, 37–38
  table saw, 32–35
Right-angle platform, 68–70
Router

dado joints, 24–28
dovetail joints, 73–80
edge joints, 14–16
lap joints, 83–89
mortise-and-tenon joints,
  98–103, 108–109
rabbet joints, 36–38
sliding dovetail joints, 63–70
splined joints, 52, 55, 59
straight bit, 14–16
tenons, 108–109

Safety notice, 2
Sliding dovetail joints, 60. *See also*
  Dovetail joints
  bits, 62
  router, 63–70
  scaling the joint, 62–63
  slotting, 63–66
  tail-cutting, 67–71
Slot cutter, 15–16
Splined joints, 9, 50
  assembly, 59
  cutting the grooves, 52–53
  edge-miter slotting fixture, 58
  grooving bevels, 54–57
  materials, 51
  router, 52, 55, 59
  table saw, 52, 53, 54–55, 56
Step-off gauge, 121
Stopped cut, 23
Stopped dado joint, 19, 23, 25, 26,
  29
Stopped rabbets, 37–38
Suppliers, 127

Table saw
  dado joints, 20–23
  edge joints, 12–13
  lap joints, 91–92
  miter joints, 40–41, 44–45
  mortise-and-tenon joints,
    104–107
  rabbet joints, 32–35
  splined joints, 52, 53, 54–55, 56
  tenons, 104–105, 107
Tenoning jig, 83
Tenons. *See also* Mortise-and-
  tenon joints
  cutting, 104–109
  loose, 111–113
  routing, 108–109
  sawing, 107
  setting up the jig, 106
  table saw, 104–105
Through dado joint, 19
Tongue-and-groove joint, 11–17

V-groove, 17